THE BRIDE'S GUIDE

THE BRIDE'S GUIDE

How To Arrange A Wonderful Wedding

Jan Arkless

RIGHT WAY

Typeset in 10^1/$_2$ on 11^1/$_2$pt Times by One & A Half Graphics.
Printed and bound in Great Britain by Cox & Wyman Ltd., Reading,
Berkshire.

The *Right Way* series is published by Elliot Right Way Books,
Brighton Road, Lower Kingswood, Tadworth, Surrey, KT20 6TD,
U.K.

For Tim and Rowena.
It's your turn next; good luck in your future together!
And thanks to Jonathan and Barbara for providing
the inspiration for this book!

ACKNOWLEDGMENTS

The following are thanked for all their patient help and information:

Rev Canon Martin Chadwick of St Mary's Church, Charlbury
Superintendent Registrar Patricia Murfitt and the staff
  of West Oxfordshire Register Office, Witney

General Register Office, Southport
General Register Office, Edinburgh
Office of Population, Censuses and Surveys, London

Mr Kenneth Broadribb for musical advice

Annabel Arkless for providing the title

Cover photograph supplied by Greg Evans International

CONTENTS

INTRODUCTION

IT'S GOING TO BE A WONDERFUL WEDDING!

It was a sunny day in May when my son Jonathan phoned from Germany where he was working, with the news that he and his lovely German girlfriend, Barbara, had decided to get married in August. My immediate reaction was, "Great! We'll book our flight tickets immediately." But then came the bombshell: "Well, actually, we'd like a traditional English wedding in the village church. Could you sort it out for us please?"

What follows is therefore based soundly on practical, hands-on experience of arranging a wedding – not just the etiquette side of who sits where and who makes the speeches, but the actual nitty gritty arrangements without which there wouldn't be anywhere to make the speeches anyway. We did it within three months, but you can take as much or as little time as you have available. Experienced 'mothers of the bride' amongst my friends and neighbours told me horror stories of weddings that had to be planned 18 months in advance. "All the suitable venues, the church and the best hotels will be booked up at least a year ahead," they all assured me, worriedly. Maybe I was just lucky! Apparently August is a quieter time for weddings than earlier in the summer, and it is the closed season for functions and corporate entertaining as so many people are away on holiday, and lots of suitable places were available.

It was a rush, of course, and quite hard work to make all the initial arrangements, but the whole affair turned out to be great fun and I enjoyed myself immensely, especially as we were eventually rewarded by a warm and sunny wedding day, a beautiful service and a happy, relaxed reception enjoyed by bride and groom, family and friends alike. (Well, as the wedding couple stayed until 11.30pm and the last guest tottered off to bed at 3.00am, I guess a good time was had by all!)

Looking back reflectively after the day, I think the biggest lesson I learnt was never assume 'someone will do it' – they usually don't! As soon as you start making the wedding arrangements, go out and purchase a ring file, a packet of dividers and a pad of punched paper. Write out all the headings that have to be organised (wedding service, reception, catering, wedding cake, flowers, photographer, etc.) and clip them into your file, ready to keep all the notes, addresses, phone and fax numbers and appointments together and easy to refer to as the arrangements go along – or, if you have a computer and the knowledge to use it, get it all down on disk. If you decide exactly how you want something done, make sure it is clearly explained to those involved, and always double check arrangements to make sure that everything will go as well and as happily as possible.

Watch the local paper for adverts for "Wedding Fayres", where there will be displays of all sorts of wedding facilities and necessities, from reception venues and car hire to wedding dresses, cakes, bouquets and floral decorations. Even if you don't avail yourself of the actual services on offer it's a good place to gather ideas or to eliminate what you don't want at your own wedding!

If you are too busy or unable to manage all the arrangements, there are wedding consultants available in most parts of the country (see adverts in bridal magazines or Yellow Pages) who will arrange the reception or organise the entire wedding if necessary.

Whoever is responsible for organising the wedding – be it the bride, the mother of the bride, the mother of the bridegroom, or even the bridegroom or one of the fathers – I hope you'll find this book and my experiences clear, helpful and amusing!

Good luck, and I hope you have a wonderful wedding.

PART ONE
Getting Married:
The Ceremony

1
LEGAL REQUIREMENTS

Once the momentous step of deciding to get married has been taken, the next big decision is about the kind of marriage ceremony that is wanted – a traditional white wedding with a religious service, a register office wedding, or the newer Civil Marriage Service. Whichever type of ceremony is chosen, the legal conditions with regard to the marriage laws and regulations are the same throughout England and Wales, although in Northern Ireland the laws are slightly different and in Scotland there is more freedom as to where the ceremony can take place.

In England and Wales the minimum age for getting married is 16, and a birth certificate must be available for proof if necessary. Anyone under 18 years of age must have written, signed permission from both parents or guardians. If the parents or guardians are abroad their written permission must be witnessed by a notary public or a consular official from the British Embassy. If the parents or guardians are deceased, or unavailable, or refuse their consent, the under 18-year-old can apply to the court for permission to marry.

There are laws forbidding marriage between close relatives, as listed in the Book of Common Prayer or at the Register Office, and the couple must generally not be of the same sex, although there is presently much discussion regarding this amongst Church, Registrars and Civil Rights Groups.

Both parties must be of sound mind and acting of their own free will. (Shotgun weddings are no longer fashionable!) If either partner has been married before, they must produce the legal documents to prove they are free to remarry. If the original partner has died, a death certificate is necessary, or if there has been a divorce, the decree absolute is required (a decree nisi is not enough), or a certificate of annulment from a former marriage. There must be at least two witnesses to the marriage (not counting the clergyman or Registrar) who must be over 18 and willing to sign the marriage register.

Getting the Licence

The couple must apply to the appropriate authority for a licence to marry. The type of licence necessary will vary according to the kind of ceremony chosen and its individual circumstances. The clergyman or Registrar will explain the kind of licence needed, how to obtain it, and the costs involved.

Marriage within the Church of England

At least one of the couple must have been baptised into the Christian faith. The marriage must take place in the parish where one, or both, of the couple live, or where they have resided long enough to fulfil the necessary legal qualifications (see below). If one or both of the couple have, for at least 6 months, worshipped regularly at a church outside the parish in which they live, they will then be entitled to sign the electoral roll of that parish, giving them the right to be married in that church.

If the couple wish to be married in any other church or chapel, unless the residential qualifications can be fulfilled, a Special Licence or Superintendent Registrar's Certificate would be needed. This may also be necessary for marriage in school or college chapels, private chapels and even certain Cathedrals which are not registered for marriage.

There are four ways in which a marriage can be authorised to take place within the Church of England:
1. by Banns
2. by Common Licence
3. by Special Licence
4. by Superintendent Registrar's Certificate.

Banns

Marriage by banns is the most usual method of marriage in the Church of England. An application should be made to the incumbent of the church in which the couple wish to be married. Only one of them need make the application, although it is usual for the couple to meet the clergyman together, with proof (if necessary) of their eligibility to marry. The date and time of the ceremony can be arranged and the banns (names of bride and groom and their intention to get married) must then be read out during a service on three consecutive Sundays in the parish(es) in which each of the couple reside (and must reside there for the full 21 days during which the banns are published). If necessary the banns must also be read in the parish church where one, or both, of the couple are on the electoral roll if the marriage is to take place there.

After the banns have been read for the three Sundays, provided that no objections to the marriage have been declared, the service can take place between 8.00am and 6.00pm, any day in the next three calendar months. If the marriage does not take place within this time, the banns will need to be called again if the marriage is still to take place. Fees are charged for calling the banns and issuing the necessary marriage licence.

Marriage by Common Licence

If there is not enough time for the banns to be called, or the couple cannot fulfil the residential qualifications needed, or one of the couple is not a British subject or is not resident in England or Wales, the marriage must take place by Common Licence. As with marriage by banns, application must be made by one, or both, of the couple to the clergyman of the church where they wish to be married.

The residential qualifications are not so strict as for banns. One of the couple needs to live in the parish where the marriage is to take place (for at least 15 days prior to the application for the licence). The other partner does not have to fulfil any residential qualifications at all. In the case of a couple where only one is a British subject, the British partner must be the one to fulfil the residential qualifications (15 days). One clear day's notice is then needed before the ceremony can take place, and the ceremony must take place within 3 calendar months of the licence being granted.

If the clergyman is not registered to grant the licence himself, he or she will be able to give the couple the address of the Surrogate or Diocesan Registrar for granting marriage licences in the Diocese, where they must apply instead. In all cases fees are charged for the issue of the Marriage Licence.

Marriage by Special Licence

Marriage by Special Licence is only allowed in exceptional circumstances, and is issued on the authority of the Archbishop of Canterbury through the Registrar of the Court of Faculties (1, The Sanctuary, London, SW1P 3JT). A Special Licence is needed when a religious marriage ceremony has to take place urgently outside a church licensed for marriage, possibly at a hospital bedside in the case of very serious illness. Some of the great British Cathedrals, including St Paul's and Westminster Abbey, are not registered for marriage, and a Special Licence is required before a marriage can take place there.

Marriage by Superintendent Registrar's Certificate within the Church of England

It is possible to be married in a church or chapel of the Church of England (possibly a school or college chapel) by authorisation of a Superintendent Registrar's Certificate, instead of by banns, but the clergyman of the church where the couple wish to marry has the right to insist that the couple apply for a Common Licence before he will marry them. At least one of the couple must fulfil the necessary residential qualifications in the parish or ecclesiastical district in which the church is situated, and the Certificate must be obtained from the Superintendent Registrar of that district. The notice to the Registrar takes the place of the banns, and both partners must apply for the issue of a Superintendent Registrar's Certificate in their appropriate districts (see below); one partner cannot apply for a Certificate and the other publish banns.

Marriage outside the Church of England

Marriage by Superintendent Registrar's Certificate

This Certificate is obtained from the Register Office in the district where the couple live or where they wish to be married. A Certificate for marriage in the register office, registered building or certain churches in that district is obtainable 21 clear days after notice of marriage has been given to the Registrar. Both partners must reside in that district for not less than 7 days prior to the serving of the notice (applying for the certificate), or, if one partner lives in another district, he or she must fulfil the 7 days' residence there and then give notice to the Registrar of that district and obtain his certificate also, which must then be presented to the Registrar or clergyman where the wedding is to take place.

If the wedding is to take place in a district where neither of the couple lives, arrangements must be made with the Registrar or clergyman in that district. Residential qualifications must still be fulfilled in the couple's own district(s) (7 days) and notice of marriage given to the Registrar(s), and the necessary certificate(s) presented to the Registrar or clergyman where the marriage is to take place.

Notice of the intended marriage is displayed during the 21 days prior to the issue of the certificate(s) in the Register Office(s) of the district(s) in which each of the couple live. Fees will be charged by all Registrars involved. Most Registrars have an appointment system for couples wishing to give notice of marriage; the phone number will be found in the telephone directory under Registration of Births, Deaths and Marriages.

Marriage by Registrar's Certificate and Licence

If the wedding is to be held at shorter notice than is possible under a Superintendent Registrar's Certificate, a licence can be obtained from the Registrar in the district where the couple live or where they wish to be married, which allows the marriage to take place only 7 clear days after the date of notice. If the couple both live in the district, one must have resided there for not less than 15 days and the other for not less than 7 days preceding the serving of notice. If one of them lives in another district, a residence of 15 days must be fulfilled there and notice given to the Registrar of that district and a certificate obtained there. The Registrar of the district where the marriage is to take place will require the certificate from the Registrar of the other district before the licence can be issued.

If the marriage is to take place in a district where neither of the couple is normally resident the necessary documents must be obtained from the Registrar(s) of the district(s) in which the couple live. Arrangements must also be made for the marriage ceremony with the Registrar of the district where they wish to be married.

Separate fees will be charged by all Registrars concerned, and in all cases the marriage must take place within 3 calendar months from the date of issue of Certificate or Licence. If not, a new application will need to be made to the Registrar(s).

2
MAKING ARRANGEMENTS FOR THE CEREMONY

Setting the Date

When deciding the wedding date, check with family and close friends to make sure that it will be possible for them to attend on that day – make sure no-one important has booked a holiday or even their own wedding then. Also check that it does not clash with an important sporting event, such as the FA Cup Final, or you may find more guests crowding round the hotel television than socialising at the reception. Obviously popular venues for both the ceremony and the reception are also booked up well in advance, and it may even be necessary to hold the wedding during the week, or on a Sunday, if that proves possible, in order to hold them at the venues of your choice.

Church Weddings

If the wedding is to take place in church, also be aware that some clergy prefer not to hold weddings during Lent (the six weeks before Easter), a solemn time in the church. Even if the clergyman allows a wedding during Lent you may find that floral decorations may not be permitted and that the bells may not be rung. At popular 'wedding times' (Easter, Bank Holidays and Saturdays in the summer), it may be necessary to book the church well ahead, especially if you want to hold the service at a particular time of day in order to fit in with arrangements for the reception.

If several weddings are taking place at the church on the same day, plenty of time needs to be allowed between the services in order to avoid any muddles of wedding guests and wedding cars, and to give all the bridal parties time to enjoy the ceremony and take photographs before and afterwards. Also, agreement will have to be reached between the brides (or their mothers) regarding the floral decorations. This is another reason some brides prefer to try and arrange a date when there are no other weddings scheduled, although if two or more brides can agree a colour scheme and share the cost of the flowers, it will be considerably cheaper for them all.

When arranging the wedding, check with the clergyman if confetti (possibly the bird friendly type) is permitted in the church yard, and if not, make sure your guests are aware of this in order to avoid any unpleasantness after the ceremony.

Most clergy like to spend a little time talking with the prospective bride and groom about the meaning of marriage and the marriage ceremony. Some churches run short courses for those about to get married in order to help couples realise that there is more to a successful marriage than a pretty wedding and a romantic honeymoon.

The clergyman will discuss the actual wedding service with the couple and plan with them the kind of service they would like. The Marriage Service in the 1662 Authorised Prayer Book is the most formal and traditional service, and uses beautiful archaic language. It includes the vow 'to obey' which does not please some brides of today, while the 1980 Alternative Service Book uses more modern language and the vow to obey is optional. This service can be conducted in a very traditional manner, or can be adapted to give the couple wider scope to make the service more personal to suit themselves. The couple may, if they wish, take Holy Communion during either version of the marriage service.

Hymns, a psalm if wished, a Bible reading and prayers will need to be chosen. The bride and groom may have their own particular favourites or may wish to incorporate special prayers, poems or vows they have written themselves. The clergyman will be able to help by suggesting a selection of hymns and readings suitable for a marriage service. When choosing hymns for a wedding, unless you are having a big choir present, or a very musical congregation, beware of including unknown or very unusual hymns, as nothing is worse than the embarrassed shuffling of a congregation that does not know the tune, while the vicar and organist try to lead the singing. The vicar will book the organist to attend and also the choir if you so wish, and will explain the fees charged for these services.

Besides the hymns, the couple must also choose the music to

be played before the service while the guests are arriving, at the entry of the bride with her father, during the signing of the register and the final procession as the bride and groom lead the wedding party from the church. The vicar will usually suggest that this is chosen in consultation with the organist, and will be able to put the couple in touch with him or her if they do not already know him through attendance at church. The couple may have musical friends or relations who will 'volunteer' to sing or play instruments during the signing of the register, giving a very personal touch to the proceedings, and this must be discussed and agreed with the vicar and the organist.

The couple may wish to ask a relative or close friend (a parent, brother, sister, aunt, uncle or cousin) who is ordained into the church, to conduct or take part in the wedding service, perhaps giving the address. This will need to be discussed and arranged with the residing cleric. If an invited clergyman conducts the service, it is usual to pay the marriage fees to the incumbent of the church, and again to the invited clergyman. A relative or friend can also be asked to read the lesson during the service.

Many couples like to have the church bells rung before and after the service. It gives a wonderful atmosphere of elation and celebration to the whole proceedings. The vicar or organist will arrange for the bell ringers to attend, and, of course, a fee is charged for their services.

The clergyman will usually suggest a rehearsal of the service in the church a few days before the actual wedding. It's a good idea for as many of the wedding retinue as possible (bridesmaids, flowergirls, pageboys, best man, ushers, bride's father and, of course, the bride's mother) to attend, in order that everyone knows what to do 'on the day'. Obviously the bride and bridesmaids will not wear their wedding attire, but little bridesmaids and flowergirls can practise carrying a posy of flowers or a little basket similar to that to be used at the ceremony, and if the bride is wearing a dress with a train, a few metres of any material can be pinned to her dress to give pageboys and bridesmaids practice at carrying and arranging it.

Music at the Service
The music played at the wedding ceremony sets the tone of the occasion, and whether bride and groom choose traditional or

contemporary music, it should be suitably stirring and joyful to
promote the mood of celebration. Church music is usually
played on the organ, the standard of which will vary according
to the instrument and the organist's ability, and this should be
borne in mind when choosing the music to be played. The
couple may like to invite a competent relative or friend to play
the organ at their wedding service, and this will have to be
agreed with the residing cleric and church organist.

Unless the couple has some particular music in mind, the
organist usually plays a selection of pieces during the 20
minutes or so while the guests are assembling, before the bride
arrives. An experienced church organist will have a wide
repertoire of suitable music, possibly to provide a soothing
background for a nervous bridegroom!

Music before the service could include:
  Trumpet Voluntary by Clarke
  Aria and Gavotte by Wesley
  Holsworthy Church Bells by Wesley
  Enigma Variations – 'Nimrod' – by Elgar
  Jesu, Joy of Man's Desiring by Bach
  Sheep May Safely Graze by Bach
  Excerpts from *Water Music* by Handel
  Aria and Gavotte by Handel
  March from Scipio by Handel
  Minuet from Berenice by Handel

Music for the bride's arrival and entry into the church
This is a very personal choice. It needs to be happy but stately,
so that the bride and her father aren't forced to run up the aisle
but can process to meet the groom at a comfortable pace.

Traditional choices include:
  Bridal March from Lohengrin by Wagner (*Here comes the
    Bride*) – very popular, the only time you'll have the
    chance to use it and both mothers will cry!
  Bridal March by Parry
  Music for the Royal Fireworks by Handel
  Arrival of the Queen of Sheba by Handel (very joyful, our
    bride's choice)

Wedding Hymns and Psalms
These are usually songs of joy and praise and there are any number of suitable hymns to be found in the church hymn book. If you want the congregation to join in and 'have a good sing', choose hymns that everyone will recognise and enjoy singing, but before choosing your favourite hymns, read the words carefully to make sure they are suitable for a wedding; 'Fight the good fight' is best avoided! If you are having the church choir to sing at the service, the organist will advise you of hymns which the choir can enhance with descant and harmonies to add to the beauty of the music. If there is no church choir available, it may be possible to arrange a choir from members of a local choral society if the vicar has no objections.

Popular wedding hymns and psalms include:
Praise, my soul, the King of Heaven
Lord of all hopefulness
Love Divine, all Loves excelling
Glorious things of Thee are spoken
The King of Love my Shepherd is
Come down, O Love Divine
Immortal, Invisible, God only wise
Lead us, Heavenly Father, lead us
Praise the Lord! Ye heavens adore Him
Now thank we all our God
Praise to the Lord, the Almighty, the King of Creation.
    (our bride's choice, sung together by 'both sides' in German or English)
The Lord's my Shepherd (Psalm 23, Crimond)
Jerusalem

During the Signing of the Register
The organist may be willing to play any suitable music of your choice at this point, either traditional wedding music or modern music which has a special meaning for the couple. If the choir is present they will usually sing a psalm or an anthem, or the couple may arrange for a friend, relation or a group to sing or play either traditional music, contemporary tunes or even a pop song, provided the words and music are suitable for the occasion and the clergyman does not object.

Traditional music played during the signing of the register includes:

Ave Maria by Gounard
Jesu, Joy of Man's Desiring by Bach
God be in my Head – traditional
Exultate Jubilate by Mozart
Laudate Dominum by Mozart
Panis Angelicus by Franck

Recessional Music
The bride and groom will want to finish the ceremony with some really joyful, or even triumphant music when they walk down the aisle together as husband and wife at the end of the service, and the organ should thunder out a glorious song of praise.

Traditional recessional music includes:

Trumpet Voluntary by Boyce
Trumpet Tune and Air by Purcell
Toccata in C by Pachelbal
Wedding March from 'A Midsummer Night's Dream' by Mendelssohn (the traditional wedding march and our bride's choice)
Toccata from Symphony No.5 by Widor

3

A TRADITIONAL CHURCH OF ENGLAND WEDDING

Arriving at the Church

It is traditional that bride and groom do not see each other on their wedding day (it's supposed to be unlucky if they do), until the bride is led up the aisle to stand beside her bridegroom for the marriage service. This means that both should have returned to their own homes before midnight the previous day. If the bride and groom are already living together they will probably make arrangements to spend the night at different addresses, and if their homes are close together they will have to be careful not to bump into each other in the street before setting off to the church.

The bridegroom, best man and ushers should arrive at the church at least 30 minutes before the service is due to start. They should be greeted by the clergyman, and any outstanding fees settled by the best man, who should also make a final check that he has got the ring(s) safely in his pocket. Buttonholes can be distributed to the ushers, and the service sheets carried down by the best man or chief usher or hymn books put ready to give out to the guests as they enter the church. The photographer should be there already, and there will be time to take some pictures before the guests start arriving. The best man should escort the bridegroom into the church when the organist starts playing, and they then take their places in the front right hand pew, with the groom next to the aisle and the best man on his right.

The ushers should greet the guests as they arrive at the church door, present them with a service sheet or hymn book and show them to a seat (bride's family and friends on the left hand side facing the altar, groom's on the right). Close family sit near the front, with distant relatives and friends further back – don't forget to leave the front left hand pew for the bride's parents and the right hand pew behind the bridegroom for his parents. If an usher does not recognise a guest, he should greet them and enquire 'Bride or groom?' before showing them to a pew on the appropriate side.

The groom's parents should arrive 15-20 minutes before the service, so that they can greet the guests as they take their places in the pew directly behind the bridegroom. The bride's mother should be the last 'guest' to arrive, 10-15 minutes before the start of the service, possibly travelling in the car with the bridesmaids, or with one of the family, having left her daughter and husband (or whoever is giving the bride away) ready to set off to the church a few minutes later. She should be escorted to her place in the front left hand pew by one of the ushers, and should sit a little in from the aisle so that she can be joined later by the bride's father. The bridesmaids and pageboys should arrive 10-15 minutes beforehand, to allow time for photographs before the bride arrives, but not so early that any young ones get bored or restless. They await the bride in the church porch. On no account should they enter the church before the bride arrives.

The bride and her father should arrive on time, having made allowances for any likely traffic hold ups on the way to the church. If the wedding car gets through the traffic faster than expected, the driver should 'cruise round the block' to ensure that the bride arrives exactly on time, and doesn't cause mayhem amongst the guests not already seated by arriving early! Care must also be taken not to arrive more than a minute or two late either, as this would be most discourteous to the waiting clergyman, organist, choir and guests, and create panic in the breast of an already nervous bridegroom, besides seriously delaying any wedding due to follow immediately afterwards. The bride will be helped from the car by the chauffeur and her father, and the chief bridesmaid will arrange the wedding dress and put any final touches needed to the veil and headdress. The bridal retinue will line up, with the bride on her father's right, followed by pageboys and flowergirls, the chief bridesmaid and the rest of the bridesmaids in pairs behind. The photographer will have been taking pictures while all this is happening, and after a few more formal poses the bride will be ready to enter the church with her father.

Sometimes the clergyman greets the bride at the church door, and precedes the bridal retinue up the aisle, or he may await her by the chancel steps with the bridegroom and best man. The choir may walk up the aisle in front of the clergyman or may have already taken their places in the choir stalls to await the bride.

The organist will be alerted that the bride is ready, and will strike up the introductory music to the chosen wedding march (and the groom will heave a big sigh of relief!). The bridegroom and best man move forward from their pew to the chancel steps, with the best man on the right of the bridegroom, and turn to welcome the bride as she approaches. The congregation rise, and the bride and her father enter, followed by the bridal retinue, and process up the aisle in time to the music (enjoy it, you should only do this once!) to take their places at the chancel steps, with the bride standing between the groom on her right and her father on her left (see figure 1).

Once they are in position the chief bridesmaid should step forward and take the bride's bouquet, and help her lift back the veil, although the bride may prefer to leave the veil forward until she goes to sign the register. The chief bridesmaid returns to her place behind the bride, checking that the rest of the retinue are in their places too. It may be more convenient to arrange for small bridesmaids and pageboys to join their parents in nearby pews while the service is taking place, and then rejoin the bridal retinue for the signing of the register.

The Ceremony
The ceremony begins with a short greeting from the clergyman, followed by a hymn, short prayers and the Bible reading. The marriage service then takes place, the exact words will depend on whether the couple have chosen the service in the 1662 Authorised Prayer Book or the 1980 Alternative Service Book. The clergyman addresses the congregation, stating the purpose of matrimony, and asks first the congregation and then the couple if they know of any impediment to the marriage. After a short pause for anyone to speak, the clergyman turns to the bridegroom and asks: 'Wilt thou have this woman to thy wedded wife, to live together according to God's law in the holy estate of matrimony? Wilt thou love her, comfort her, honour and keep her in sickness and in health; and forsaking all other, keep thee only unto her, so long as ye both shall live?' The man answers: 'I will.'

The clergyman then asks the bride the same questions and the woman answers: 'I will.'

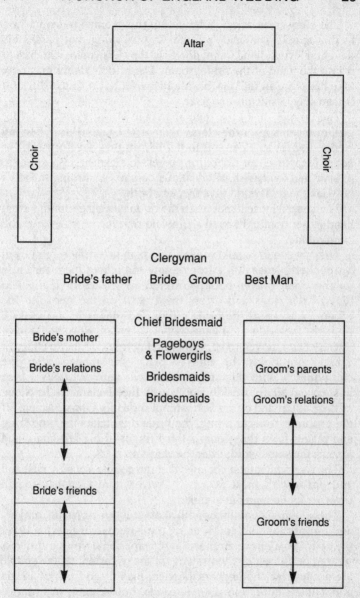

Figure 1: During the ceremony

The clergyman asks: 'Who giveth this woman to be married to this man?' The bride's father says nothing, but passes his daughter's right hand, palm down, to the clergyman, who passes it into the hand of the bridegroom. The bride's father may now take his place in the pew beside his wife, but if this is difficult he can stay beside his daughter.

The couple then take their marriage vows. First the bridegroom repeats after the clergyman: 'I *** take thee *** to my wedded wife, to have and to hold from this day forward, for better for worse, for richer for poorer, in sickness and in health, to love and to cherish, till death us do part, according to God's holy law; and thereto I give thee my troth.'

The couple loose hands, then the bride takes the groom's right hand in her own right hand again, and repeats the vows after the clergyman.

They free their hands, and the best man takes the ring(s) from his pocket (please don't drop them!) and places them carefully on the open prayer book proffered by the clergyman, who blesses the rings and offers them, still on the book, to the groom, who takes the bride's ring and places it on the third finger of the bride's left hand (her engagement ring should have already been moved to her right hand before coming to church). The groom holds the ring in place and repeats after the clergyman: 'With this ring I thee wed, with my body I thee honour and all my worldly goods with thee I share: In the Name of the Father, and of the Son, and of the Holy Ghost. Amen.' If the groom is to wear a ring, the bride then takes the other ring and places it on the groom's third finger of his left hand, and repeats the same words after the clergyman.

The clergyman then declares that the couple are now husband and wife, with these words: 'These whom God has joined together let no man put asunder.'

The ceremony continues with another hymn or psalm, prayers and a short address, and if using the Alternative Service Book the couple may have arranged to repeat special vows or prayers written or chosen by themselves for the occasion. (If the couple are not regular churchgoers the vicar may try to find out a little about them both, and their families, beforehand, in order to make the address more personal and appropriate to the occasion.) This concludes the official part of the service, and the bride and groom follow the clergyman to the altar steps where they kneel to receive the Nuptial Blessing, and some couples may have arranged to take Holy Communion together for the first time as husband and wife.

The clergyman leads the way to the vestry or side chapel, followed in procession by the bride and groom, the bridal retinue, best man, groom's father escorting bride's mother, and bride's father with groom's mother, and occasionally other relatives, perhaps grandparents. In the vestry the bride signs the register using her maiden name for probably the last time (although legally she may choose whether to take her husband's surname or not), followed by the bridegroom, the clergyman and the two witnesses (best man, chief bridesmaid, father, mother or whoever has been previously asked to do so). While this is happening the congregation sit and listen to the music provided by the organist, choir or special guest performer(s). A copy of the entry in the church register (marriage certificate) paid for earlier by the groom is given to the bride before they leave the vestry, and she gives these 'Marriage Lines' to her husband to keep safely in an inner pocket.

The bride now lifts back her veil if she has not previously done so, and the chief bridesmaid hands back her bouquet. The organist gets a signal from the clergyman and breaks into the triumphal wedding march, as the groom proudly leads his bride back down the aisle on his left arm (leaving his right, sword arm free to defend her if necessary!), followed by pageboys and bridesmaids. The best man escorts the chief bridesmaid, followed by the parents, as before (see figure 2). If there are any little flowergirls, they will walk ahead of the bride and groom, strewing flowers from their baskets as they go (*if* this has been agreed with the vicar!).

The photographer will be waiting at the church door (having hared back from the vestry where he will have photographed the signing of the register), to capture the moment the couple emerge from the church as husband and wife, and then there will be time for formal group photos and informal pictures of the bridal group. Wedding guests will also want some time to take photographs and there will probably be a lot of people who want to chat with relatives and friends they 'only meet at weddings'. The bride's parents will want a few moments to thank the clergyman, and, through him, the organist, choir and bellringers, whether he is attending the reception or not.

'Someone' (bride's mother, father or the best man) needs to keep a check on the time, in order to get everyone to the reception by the arranged time, and to clear the church if there is another wedding party due.

The wedding car or carriage will draw up to the church, and the bride and groom leave first in a traditional hail of confetti (but check this out with the vicar beforehand). The bridesmaids, flowergirls and pageboys leave next in the pre-arranged transport, followed by the parents of the bride and groom who need to get to the reception ahead of the guests in order to greet everyone as they arrive. The wedding guests then make their own way to the reception, and the ushers leave last, having made sure that everyone has got a lift to the reception, everyone knows where it is being held, and everyone knows how to get there!

Guard of Honour

A Guard of Honour may be formed at the church door to welcome the newly weds as they come out of the church at the end of the service. The Guard of Honour may be a military guard, if either bride or groom is a member of, or has family connections with, one of the services, or it may be formed by members of the bride or groom's profession or colleagues from work, or by members of a club or society to which either of the couple belongs. The guard may wait outside during the service, or sit at the back of the church and slip out unobtrusively during the signing of the register and line up in pairs to form a series of arches with military swords, oars, hockey sticks, cricket bats, wooden spoons, rolling pins, document tubes, etc, or any appropriate symbol of club or profession (let your imagination run riot!) under which the couple will pass as they emerge from the church. The Guard of Honour is usually arranged for the couple by their colleagues or club members, often as a surprise as they come out of church.

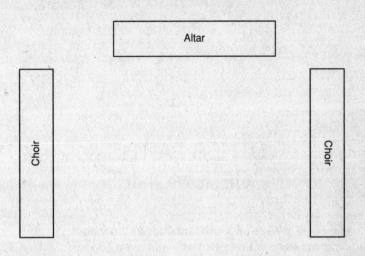

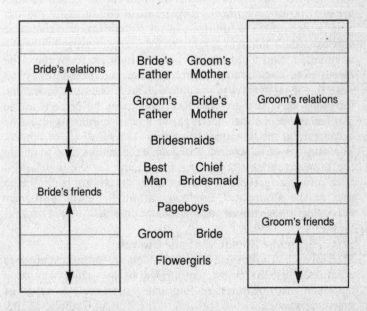

Figure 2: Leaving the church

4

OTHER FAITHS & CEREMONIES

Marriage in Free or Non-Conformist Churches
In the majority of Protestant denominations (Baptist, Methodist, United Reform, etc.) the church building itself is registered by the Superintendent Registrar as a building in which marriages may be solemnised, and many of the ministers of these churches are registered as 'authorised' persons to conduct and register marriages, so that weddings can take place there in the same way as in the Church of England. Occasionally, particularly in a very small Non-Conformist church which may not have the facilities to keep its own church register, the minister may not have this legal authority, and although he or she can conduct the religious service there, the Registrar must be present at the service to record the marriage, or a civil ceremony must be conducted at the Register Office prior to a religious ceremony. The minister of the church will advise the couple how to obtain the Superintendent Registrar's Certificate for the marriage if necessary (see page 14). The wedding ceremony is similar to that of the Church of England, although details will vary according to the rites of each particular church.

Marriage in the Roman Catholic Church
Marriages can take place in most Roman Catholic churches conducted by the priest, authorised in the same way as a marriage in the Church of England. There are two types of marriage service within the rites of the Roman Catholic church – 'Marriage Celebrated during Mass' and 'Marriage Celebrated outside Mass'. Mass can only be celebrated during a marriage

when both bride and groom are baptised into the Roman
Catholic faith. A 'mixed marriage', between a Catholic and a
baptised member of another Christian faith, requires permission
from the Catholic partner's parish priest, while marriage with a
non-baptised person needs a special dispensation, also
obtainable from the parish priest. In both cases the Catholic will
have to promise to do everything possible to stay within the
faith and to ensure the Catholic baptism and upbringing of all
children of the marriage. The priest must be able to sign a
statement that in his opinion the non-Catholic will not oppose
these promises. However, in these enlightened times with much
more talk of unity between the Christian churches, there is more
understanding of the difficulties regarding a 'mixed marriage',
and many priests will be most supportive and do all they can to
accommodate any 'mixed' couple who wish to get married in
the Roman Catholic Church, once it has been established that
the non-Catholic does not wish to convert to Roman
Catholicism.

The priest will usually ask the couple to attend some form of
religious instruction to prepare them for marriage. He will
explain the legal requirements and how to make arrangements
for the Registrar to attend if necessary (see Free Church
Weddings, page 30). The marriage ceremony is similar to that of
the Church of England but is conducted according to the rites of
the Roman Catholic Church.

Quakers (Religious Society of Friends)
A Quaker marriage is completely different from most other
wedding services. It is very beautiful, simple and quite free of
any ceremonial. It is not an alternative form of marriage
available to the general public, but is restricted to Quaker
members and those associated with them, so therefore at least
one of the couple must belong or be known to the local Quaker
meeting. Application must be made, at least 6 weeks before the
proposed wedding date, to the Registering Officer of the
monthly meeting where the couple usually worship or where
they wish the marriage to take place. A non-Quaker application
must obtain support in writing from 2 adult members of the
Society, given on forms which the Registering Officer will
supply. If the Registering Officer assents to the application he
will supply the appropriate forms for the Superintendent

Registrar. The couple must then make application to marry, in accordance with civil law, to the Superintendent Registrar of Marriages (see page 14). Notice of the intended marriage is given by the Quaker Registering Officer at the Sunday morning meeting(s) to which the couple belong or which they usually attend, or in the area in which they live or wish to marry. If no written objection is received, the Registering Officer will ask the appropriate meeting to appoint a Meeting for Worship for the Solemnisation of Marriage. Public notice of such a meeting will be given at the place at which it is to be held, at the close of the previous meeting for worship.

The Marriage Service, as any Quaker meeting, is held on the basis of silent communion of the spirit: there is no pageantry, music, set service or sermon, but there is opportunity for those who feel moved by the spirit to give a spoken prayer. The bride generally wears a plain or quite simple wedding dress, and it is unusual for the groom to wear a morning suit. It is not necessary for the couple to be attended by a bridesmaid or a best man. There is no processional entry, the bride and groom simply take their places with the rest of the meeting. When they feel ready, the couple rise and, hand in hand, make their declaration of marriage. The bridegroom says: 'Friends, I take this my friend *** to be my wife, promising through divine assistance to be unto her a loving and faithful husband, so long as we both on earth shall live.' The bride makes a similar declaration.

The marriage certificate is then signed by bride and groom and two of the witnesses. The certificate is read aloud by the Registering Officer, and after the meeting it is usual for all those present to sign the certificate also. The wedding ring plays no official part in the marriage service, although the couple often exchange rings later in the meeting, or the groom gives one to his bride. At the end of the meeting the couple withdraw with four witnesses and the Registering Officer to complete the civil marriage register, but there is no bridal procession.

The Jewish Marriage
Before the religious side of the marriage can be arranged, the bride and groom must obtain a Superintendent Registrar's Certificate from the Register Office in the district(s) in which they live (see page 14). They must then apply for the Chief Rabbi's authorisation, which can be arranged by their local

minister or secretary for meetings, or directly from the Chief Rabbi's office, giving at least three weeks' notice before the wedding is due to take place.

Although Jewish weddings are usually held in a Synagogue, they are permitted to take place anywhere (private house, garden, hotel, hall, etc.) as long as they still take place under a chuppah (wedding canopy). The ceremony can be held at any time, excluding the Jewish Sabbath (sunset on Friday to sunset on Saturday) or any Festival or Fast Day, and it is unusual for weddings to take place on the eves of Sabbaths or Festivals.

On the wedding day it is customary for the bride and groom to fast until after the ceremony. The groom arrives for the ceremony first and sits in the Warden's Box with his father, best man and future father-in-law. When the bride arrives, the groom takes his place under the chuppah and the best man stands behind to his left. The bride is now usually brought in by her father, followed by the bridesmaids, the bride's mother escorted by a male relative, and the groom's parents, or the bride may choose to follow the old Jewish custom and be brought in by her mother and future mother-in-law. Before the bride stands under the chuppah the groom is asked to approve the 2 witnesses and accept the terms of the Ketubah (marriage document), where he promises to undertake various obligations to the bride. The bride then comes under the chuppah standing on the groom's right, with both sets of parents by their children, and the wedding service proceeds with blessings of betrothal over a cup of wine.

In Jewish law the couple are married when the man places the ring on the woman's finger, with the acceptance of the ring signifying her consent. This act is carried out by the bride and groom themselves, as it is not the minister who marries them, but the couple who marry each other, the minister being present as a Jewish law expert and in a civil capacity as Secretary for Marriages. The ring must be of precious metal without any jewels, and is placed on the bride's right index finger (used symbolically to acquire things), although she may transfer it to her left hand ring finger later. The groom recites in Hebrew 'Behold thou art consecrated unto me by this ring according to the laws of Moses and Israel', implying that the requirements of Jewish law have been met. The Ketubah is now read, in Aramaic and English and given to the bride to keep safely.

Prayers for the seven blessings of marriage follow and the bridal pair sip from a cup of wine together, to symbolise that they will share the same cup of life. The groom then shatters the glass and a final blessing is given. The couple and the witnesses sign the marriage documents. The bride and groom then lead the bridal procession from the synagogue.

Register Office Wedding

The marriage ceremony at a Register Office is shorter and more businesslike than most religious ceremonies, but can still be arranged formally, as for a church wedding, with the bride wearing a traditional white wedding dress and attended by bridesmaids. She can arrive at the Register Office on her father's arm, where the bridegroom, best man and as many guests as there is room for in the office, will be waiting. On the other hand, the wedding can be a very informal occasion, attended only by the bride and groom, the Registrar and two witnesses who need not even know the couple but happen to be in the building. Most couples opt for the happy medium, with the actual ceremony being attended only by the families and very close friends, due to lack of space in the Register Office, followed by a traditional wedding reception for other relatives and friends.

The couple must make arrangements for the marriage with the Superintendent Registrar of the actual Register Office where they wish to marry. Since the introduction of the new Marriage Act in 1995, couples are now allowed to marry in any Register Office of their choice (some offices are in pleasanter settings than others) without necessarily having to fulfil residential qualifications in that district.

A *provisional* booking for the date and time of the wedding can be made up to one year in advance, although formal notice and a confirmed booking cannot be made earlier than three months prior to the date of marriage. The couple must first obtain a Superintendent Registrar's Certificate or Certificate and Licence from the Register Office(s) in the district(s) where they live (see pages 14-15), and when this has been issued they can make formal arrangements for the marriage with the Registrar of the office where they want to get married. The Superintendent Registrar has no legal right to refuse to remarry a divorced person, provided the decree absolute has been granted and all other legal requirements have been met, as civil law takes no cognisance of religious beliefs or scruples in such cases.

When the couple arrive for the marriage, the Registrar will explain the proceedings to them in private, and any outstanding fees are paid. The guests then join them for the ceremony, which begins with a short address by the Registrar. The couple exchange their vows to each other, repeating in turn: 'I do solemnly declare that I know not of any lawful impediment why I ** may not be joined in matrimony to **'. They then say to one another in turn: 'I call upon these persons here present to witness that I ** take thee ** to be my lawful wedded husband (or wife).' This must be said in front of the two witnesses. The register is signed by the newly weds, the two witnesses and the Registrar. The exchange of wedding rings by bride and groom is common practice, but has no legal significance under civil law.

The marriage service *may not* include anything religious whatsoever; sacred readings, music, hymns or prayers are not allowed, but the Registrar will usually try to arrange the service to suit an individual couple, to make it a special day for them, and will discuss any secular readings or poems the couple would like to include, or promises written by the couple to each other. Non-religious music may be included (but the couple will have to arrange it themselves) if the Registrar is agreeable, but it must be remembered that the Register Office is usually very busy, especially on Fridays and Saturdays, and there just may not be time for any additions to the civil service.

Photography is not usually allowed during the ceremony, but some photographs can be taken at the end of the service (bearing in mind there may be another wedding party waiting), and more photographs can be taken outside the Register Office afterwards.

Service of Blessing
This often follows soon after a Register Office ceremony, possibly when the couple have been unable to marry in church because one or both of them have been divorced. The service often takes place before a reception, and is attended by all the relatives and friends of the couple who were unable to attend the civil ceremony due to lack of space in the Register Office. Occasionally a couple who have been married abroad or in a

distant part of the country, or for some reason their actual wedding was a very quiet affair (perhaps due to a bereavement or work commitments), may arrange for a Service of Blessing to which they can invite all those who were unable to attend the wedding earlier. In this case the bride may choose to wear her wedding dress again, and be attended by her bridesmaids as at the original ceremony, or she can wear her 'going away' outfit or an entirely new outfit bought for the occasion. It must, however, be made clear to the guests that this is not an actual marriage service.

A Service of Blessing is held entirely at the discretion of the clergyman concerned, although most clergy will give more sympathetic consideration to conducting this service when a divorced person is involved even if they are not prepared to perform the actual marriage service in the church. The service has no legal formalities and is not recorded in the church marriage register. It takes a different form entirely from the marriage ceremony, and must not pretend to be a wedding, even though the service may be followed by a traditional wedding reception. The guests assemble in the church and await the arrival of the bride and groom. The bride is not escorted into church or given away by her father, but bride and groom enter the church and walk up the aisle together, followed by the bridal retinue, if there is one. The service can follow a formal pattern, with traditional wedding music, hymns, Bible reading and prayers, or the couple may choose to include music, poems and prayers that they have written themselves or have a special meaning for them.

The service does not have to take place in a church although this is most usual, but can be held before the reception at home, in the hotel, hall, marquee or even in the garden, according to the wishes of the bride and groom, provided the clergyman is willing to officiate.

A Double Wedding
This is the marriage of two couples before the same clergyman (or Superintendent Registrar), at the same time in the same ceremony. In this case the brides are usually sisters or the grooms are brothers, often twins, or sister and brother may marry different partners.

A double wedding entails the same legal arrangements as must be made for any marriage, each couple obtaining their own separate licence to marry, and a separate marriage certificate will be issued to each couple. The brides will decide whether to wear matching wedding dresses, and usually have their own bridesmaids and bridal retinues. The bridegrooms usually both wear either morning or lounge suits, and each groom is supported by his own best man.

In a church the brides walk up the aisle with their father(s) to join their waiting grooms, and stand side by side before the clergyman, each bride on the left of her bridegroom. The single ceremony embraces both couples, but the responses and vows are made individually. After signing the register, due to the narrowness of most church aisles, the couples and their retinues walk down the aisle in separate parties. 'Who goes first' must be decided beforehand; there are no rules, but usually the elder bridegroom leads the way, with the younger couple following.

A double wedding is followed by a joint reception, with one top table if there is a sit down meal. However, there will be two cakes – one for each couple to cut – and speeches from the fathers of both brides (if appropriate), both bridegrooms and both of the best men.

Civil Marriage Ceremony

Since the 1994 Marriage Act (England and Wales) became law in April 1995, civil (non-religious) marriage ceremonies are allowed to take place in approved, registered premises other than Register Offices, such as hotels, stately homes, castles, historic monuments, civic buildings or night clubs. However, the new act still does not allow marriages in England and Wales to take place outside, whether in a garden, stadium, field, on a mountain or a beach (even if the actual ceremony would take place in a marquee), in a boat unless it is immovable (permanently moored) and the ceremony takes place inside in a public room, or in any other 'exotic' location such as a ship at sea, an aeroplane, hot air balloon, fun fair or in any premises not open or available to the general public. Redundant churches will not be approved, as civil marriage may not take place in any building with a religious connection, past or present. Trustees, owners or managers of suitable premises can apply to their local authority to have their premises approved and licensed for civil marriages. The Registrar General for England and Wales has stated that 'Marriage is a solemn event and must be conducted in seemly and dignified surroundings' [Office of Population Censuses and Surveys press release], and approval for registration will only be given when the premises satisfy these criteria.

The new regulations stress that the allocated 'Wedding Room' must be in a permanent structure (not a marquee) with a postal address, and open to the general public free of charge. (Clubs applying to hold weddings on their premises will have to be able to admit the general public without charge on wedding days.) The room where the ceremony is to take place must be separate from any other activities happening on the premises at the same time, and no food or drink may be sold or consumed in the Wedding Room for at least an hour before or during the ceremony. The application for registration must be made by a responsible person, who must be on duty at the premises for each wedding. Local authorities consider each application submitted and inspect the premises. Notice of such application must be published in the local press, and 21 days allowed for any objections, before the application can be approved. The approval is granted initially for three years, but can be revoked at any time if changes are made to the premises or the local authority considers them no longer suitable.

The local authority sets the fees for approving and registering the premises (paid by the owners or trustees), and for the attendance of the two Registrars necessary to conduct the marriage (normally paid by the bride and groom, unless a 'package deal' is offered by the chosen venue which includes these fees). Two Registrars must attend a civil marriage outside a Register Office, one to perform the ceremony and one to see to the legal paperwork involved. The fees for their time and services are considerably higher than for a marriage ceremony in a Register Office. Application for approval of private premises for a 'one off' wedding in their own home by a couple or their parents is not likely to be considered by the local authority, as the house would not usually be open to the general public, unless it is already open as a 'stately home'.

Couples wishing to find suitable venues for their wedding can get a list of approved premises in their area from the local Register Office or their local authority (County, Metropolitan, District or London Borough Council) and the office of the

Registrar General in Birkdale, Southport, will be able to supply a list of all approved premises throughout England and Wales.

When the venue for the wedding has been chosen, the couple must make an appointment at the Register Office of the district where the wedding will take place, to discuss the necessary arrangements with the Superintendent Registrar and to make sure that two Registrars will be available to attend and conduct the wedding. If the wedding is to take place on a Saturday or a popular 'Wedding Time' (St. Valentine's Day, Easter or Bank Holiday), booking may need to be made well in advance, particularly if the wedding venue is some distance from the Register Office, and it may be necessary to compromise on the date and/or time of the ceremony in order to fit in with the Registrar's schedule. The couple have to apply for a Superintendent Registrar's Certificate for the marriage from the district(s) where they live (see page 14) and present it to the Registrar of the district where the marriage will take place, if it is in a different district.

The marriage ceremony conducted by the Registrar is the same legal ceremony that takes place in a Register Office (see page 34) but can be more leisurely and romantic than in the office, where other couples may be queueing up outside for their wedding slot. Provided the Registrar is agreeable the couple can add to the service, music, poetry, prose, vows and promises that have a special meaning for them, as long as everything is of a *non-religious* nature. The ceremony can be as formal or casual as the couple wish, and they can arrange it to suit themselves. The traditional bride can arrive with her father who will escort her to her bridegroom in the wedding room, where the wedding guests are waiting, or the couple may choose to arrive and enter the wedding room together when the guests have assembled, or they may decide to be there first and greet the guests as they arrive for the ceremony.

This Civil Ceremony is a very recent innovation, so there are no hard and fast rules as to how the ceremony should be conducted (apart from the brief legal proceedings). The couple therefore have the opportunity to plan their wedding ceremony according to their own wishes, provided the marriage takes place indoors, is conducted by the Registrar, does not have any religious connotations and complies with the Marriage Laws and Regulations. (Religious marriage ceremonies conducted by a clergyman must still take place within a religious building and may not take place at a registered civil venue.) The new 'Civil Marriage Act' does not apply in Scotland, and civil ceremonies there must still take place within a Register Office.

Marriage of Widows and Widowers
If either or both partners have been widowed, there is no restriction on remarriage in either church or Register Office. A marriage licence must be obtained and arrangements made in the appropriate way according to the type of ceremony chosen. A church ceremony can be as traditional or informal as the couple wish. If the groom is a widower but it is the bride's first marriage, she may wish to have a traditional white wedding with wedding dress, veil and bridesmaids, and the groom may wear topper and tails. If the bride has been married before, the couple may prefer a less formal ceremony, with the bride wearing a suit or dress and pretty hat and the groom in a lounge suit for the occasion, although there is no reason why the bride may not wear a traditional wedding dress if she so wishes. The bride can be given away by her father or other (usually male) relative, or, at the marriage of an older couple, she can be given away by an adult son, or this part of the ceremony can be omitted. The couple should discuss their feelings about the ceremony with the clergyman involved, in order to make it a happy and memorable occasion for them both. A Register Office ceremony is the same, whether it is a first or second wedding.

Marriage Between Partners of Different Religions
'Mixed' Marriage (mixed religions)
If a bride and groom belong to different *Protestant* churches, Church of England, Wales or Scotland, or the Free (Non-Conformist) churches – Baptist, Methodist or United Reform Churches – there should be no problem in arranging a religious marriage service within any of these churches.

If one partner is *Roman Catholic*, although it is no longer necessary for the non-Catholic partner to convert to the Roman Catholic faith, the Catholic partner will need permission from the Parish priest to enter a 'mixed' marriage (see page 31). Nuptial mass may not be celebrated during a 'mixed' marriage ceremony. A Protestant can marry a Roman Catholic in a

Protestant church, but the Catholic will need to obtain a special dispensation from the Roman Catholic bishop.

The Society of Friends accepts non-members in a 'mixed' marriage as long as they agree with the nature of Quaker marriage. Support in writing for the non-Quaker must be obtained from two adult members of the Society before the marriage can take place.

If a Christian wants to Marry a Non-Christian
In this situation a religious ceremony can be difficult to arrange. The *Church of Rome* and some *Protestant* churches do not allow such a ceremony and in other denominations the minister would have to be convinced that *both* partners accepted and understood the Christian faith before agreeing to marry them.

The Jewish faith does not subscribe to 'mixed' marriages, and in most cases the couple would not be able to marry with a religious ceremony, unless the non-Jewish partner was willing to convert to Judaism, which involves much tuition and study and would take a considerable time.

A *'mixed' Islamic marriage* would almost certainly involve the non-Muslim converting to the Islamic faith and taking a Muslim name before the ceremony could take place. If a Muslim wished to marry a Christian in a Christian church, the marriage would not be likely to be recognised by the Islamic authorities, and there would have to be much discussion with the Christian clergy involved before such a marriage could take place.

'Mixed' Civil Marriage
Religion in any form is not allowed at all during a civil ceremony, either in a Register Office or at a Registered Venue, so couples of any religion, both Christian and/or non-Christian, can be married by the Registrar, provided the legal conditions for the marriage have been fulfilled by both partners. Some religions may not recognise a 'mixed religion' civil ceremony (or even a civil marriage ceremony at all), but the couple will be legally married according to the laws of the land.

5

RE-MARRIAGE FOR DIVORCEES

Civil Remarriage
The law of England and Wales recognises a divorced person as
single (and so free to marry) as long as they have a decree
absolute – a decree nisi is not enough and the couple must wait
until the decree absolute is issued before making legal arrangements to marry. Having produced that document to the
Superintendent Registrar, a remarriage in a Register Office or at
a Registered Civil Venue is conducted on exactly the same
conditions, by Superintendent Registrar's Certificate or Licence
(see pages 14-15), as for those applying with regard to a first
marriage.

Church of England
Despite a great deal of discussion on this subject, the Church of
England still officially disapproves of remarriage of a divorced
person during the lifetime of a previous partner. A clergyman
has the legal right to refuse to marry in church anyone whose
previous partner is still alive, irrespective of whether the person
concerned is the injured or guilty party, and the clergyman
cannot be compelled to permit such a marriage to take place in
his/her church, or to conduct a service for anyone who has
remarried under civil law. However, many clergy are
sympathetic to divorcees who wish to remarry, and will agree to
conduct a marriage service in church, although others will
prefer to hold a Service of Blessing in the church after a civil
marriage service has taken place in the Register Office, instead
of holding a religious marriage service.
Strictly speaking, a Service of Blessing involving divorced

persons should be quiet and private, subject to the regulations issued by the General Synod. However, at the discretion of the clergyman it can be a much grander affair, attended by a church full of wedding guests if the couple so wish – usually all the friends and relatives who could not attend the civil ceremony at the Register Office due to lack of space, although it must be made clear to everyone that this is not in fact a marriage service.

The Roman Catholic Church
The views of the Roman Catholic church on remarriage are very firm. Officially civil divorce is not recognised by the Church of Rome, although in particular circumstances it may be possible to have the first marriage of either partner annulled. If a divorced person wishes to marry in the Roman Catholic faith, the couple should discuss it with the parish priest who will advise what can be done. The Church of Rome does not recognise the right of the civil authorities to dissolve a religious marriage through divorce, therefore there can usually be no religious remarriage when there is still a surviving partner.

However, if a Catholic was married outside the Roman Catholic church (in another faith or a civil ceremony) and that marriage was not recognised by the Church of Rome, remarriage within the Catholic church may be permitted. If a previous Roman Catholic marriage was annulled by the Catholic Marriage Tribunal, remarriage will be allowed within the Church of Rome, provided the couple have the legal right to marry in civil law, by being single, or divorced by the state from their partner(s).

Free Churches
While divorce is obviously not encouraged by the Free Churches, a divorced person(s) wishing to remarry in church may be received more sympathetically by the Free Church members than by the clergy of the established churches. The question of remarriage is very much at the discretion of each particular minister, some of whom believe that the original marriage contract is binding for life, while others may accept that the wronged party of a divorce is being unjustly penalised. Others will consider that everyone is entitled to another chance.

A couple wishing to marry in church when one or both are divorced will need to discuss their case with the minister of the church where they would like to marry. In some cases it may be necessary almost to 'shop around' in order to find a minister willing to marry them.

Society of Friends

The Quakers believe in the sanctity and life long nature of marriage, but recognise that in certain circumstances it may be right to make a fresh start. The Monthly Meeting would need to be satisfied that the divorced person(s) wishing to marry there was well known to them and associated with the meeting, and it would not be willing to consider the question of re-marriage without all the circumstances being taken into account. Permission to remarry at a Friends' Meeting could then be granted at the discretion of the Monthly Meeting.

The Jewish Religion

Remarriage of a divorced person within a religious ceremony can usually be arranged, provided the necessary civil legal conditions have been fulfilled (see page 32) and the authorisation of the Chief Rabbi is obtained.

Scotland

The only difference between remarriage in England (and Wales) and Scotland concerns the method of divorce. In Scotland there is no such thing as a preliminary pronouncement or decree nisi. The decree is absolute, or final, from the moment of divorce, leaving the divorced person(s) free to arrange to remarry immediately if they so desire. Remarriage for a divorced person within a religious ceremony could be more difficult to arrange, and the couple would need to discuss this with the clergy of the church where they wished to be married.

6

MARRIAGE IN SCOTLAND, IRELAND & ABROAD

Marriage in Scotland

Both partners must be at least 16 years old, but parental consent is not required for those under 18. The rules forbidding marriage between close relatives and rules in regard to remarriage apply as in England and Wales.

Residence in the district in which you wish to be married is not required, but both prospective bride and groom must complete and sign a Marriage Notice (obtainable from any Register Office in Scotland), and take or send it to the Registrar of the district where they want to be married, who issues Marriage Schedules (licences) for both religious and civil marriages. To prove they are both eligible to marry, the couple may both need to produce birth certificates, and if either has been married before, a decree absolute (a decree nisi is not acceptable) or a certificate of annulment, or, if widowed, the death certificate of a previous spouse. At least 15 days' notice of a marriage is legally required but, in order to allow time for checks on documentation, notice of 4-6 weeks is preferable. The marriage Schedule will then be issued by the Registrar.

Marriage in the Church of Scotland

The couple should first approach the minister of the church in which they wish to be married to make arrangements, and then complete the notice of marriage and submit it to the Registrar with all the necessary documents. The Marriage Schedule will be issued by the Registrar *not more than 7 days before the wedding, and must be collected by the prospective bride or groom themselves*. (It will not be issued to even a close relative.)

The marriage Schedule must then be given to the minister performing the marriage before the ceremony. At the end of the marriage service the Schedule must be signed by the bride and groom, two witnesses who are over 16 and the minister taking the service. The completed Schedule must be returned to the Registrar within 3 days, in order that the marriage can be registered.

In Scotland the rules in regard to religious wedding venues are not so strict as in England and Wales, and religious wedding ceremonies can take place both in church or anywhere outside, including mountain tops and beaches, provided the clergyman and two witnesses are willing and able to reach the venue with the bride and groom. Any couple who really want to be married outdoors can arrange to fulfil the residential qualifications and get married in Scotland, but when planning an outdoor wedding, whether in a garden, on a beach or mountain top, or beside a loch, account must be taken of the Scottish climate!

Marriage within Other Denominations
A religious marriage, whether Roman Catholic, Free Church, Quaker, Jewish, Muslim or any other denomination, may only be solemnised by a minister, priest or other person entitled to do so under the Marriage Act (Scotland) 1977. A couple wishing to marry within these denominations should consult the incumbent of the appropriate church in order to make the arrangements.

Civil Marriage
The couple must arrange the place, date and time of the marriage ceremony with the Registrar of the district in which they wish to marry. A Marriage Notice and necessary documentation must be submitted to the Registrar at least 15 days before the marriage, but it will not be necessary to collect the Marriage Schedule beforehand, as the Registrar will bring it to the marriage ceremony. After the ceremony, when the Schedule has been signed and witnessed, the Registrar will register the marriage.

Fees
The clergyman or Registrar will explain the costs.

Marriage in Ireland

The legal requirements and regulations regarding marriage in Northern Ireland and the Irish Republic are similar to those in England and Wales, although in the Republic consent to the marriage must be obtained from parents or guardians of those under 21 years old, not 18 as elsewhere.

Religious Marriages

There are many, many forms and disciplines of the Christian Church in Ireland, all with their own rites and regulations regarding marriage. A couple wishing to marry should therefore apply to the clergy of the church where they wish the ceremony to take place, who will be able to inform them of the necessary legal regulations and religious formalities that must be completed before the wedding can take place, according to the rites of that particular church. Copies of the notice of marriage must be sent to the clergyman of the place of worship attended by each of the couple.

Civil Marriage

When a couple wish to be married without any religious ceremony, they must apply to the Registrar at the Register Office where they wish to be married.

The Registrar will explain the regulations regarding the issue of a Registrar's Certificate or Licence necessary before a civil wedding can take place. Since couples planning a civil marriage may not attend any place of worship, the notice of marriage must be advertised in a local newspaper (at the couple's expense) so that it appears at least once a week for two consecutive weeks, before the necessary Certificate or Licence for the marriage can be issued.

Marriage to a Foreign National or Marriage Abroad

Marriage laws and regulations differ for foreign nationals marrying in the UK, and for British subjects marrying abroad. Also, when a British subject (man or woman) marries a foreign national, the woman's nationality after marriage must be confirmed, as well as the nationality of any present or future children of the marriage. A British subject intending to marry a foreign national in the UK should consult the clergyman of the church in which they wish to marry, regarding the legal formalities to be fulfilled in accordance with the civil law. If the couple wish to have a civil wedding (either in a Register Office or a Registered Venue), they should consult the Registrar of the district where the marriage is to take place, and the Registrar(s) of the district(s) where they both live, if different, in order to complete the necessary legal formalities.

If a British subject wishes to marry abroad, he or she should consult the appropriate department of the British Embassy or Consulate of the country or district where the marriage is to take place, irrespective of whether both partners are British or one is a national of the country concerned. A marriage ceremony performed in many countries abroad will be recognised as legally binding in the UK, provided the necessary regulations are fulfilled, but in some countries outside Europe, particularly those farther afield in Africa, South America and the Middle and Far East, it may be necessary or advisable to have a civil and/or religious ceremony within the confines of the British Embassy or Consulate, in order to avoid any problems later regarding the legality of the marriage.

Similarly, a foreign national wishing to marry in the UK, whether to a British subject or someone of their own or other nationality, should consult his or her Embassy, consulate or resident representative in Britain, to make sure that their marriage will be accepted in their own country.

'Marriage in Paradise'

This is growing in popularity each year, with more and more couples, especially those arranging a second or even a third marriage, choosing to travel to a 'Tropical Paradise', whether the Bahamas, Caribbean, Gambia, the Kenyan coast, the Seychelles, or even farther afield, for their wedding. Many holiday companies offer 'Special Wedding Packages' where everything is arranged, including flights to and from 'Paradise', the two weeks' 'honeymoon' (usually taken before the wedding to allow time for the necessary residential qualifications!), the Marriage Licence and Registrar's services, flowers, music, photographer, champagne, wedding cake and confetti. The marriage generally takes place in a 'Wedding Bower' in the hotel garden beside the beach, usually in full view of the other holidaymakers enjoying themselves in the hotel pool.

Some couples take their families and wedding retinue with them from home to help celebrate their wedding, but most go alone and have to rely on the other hotel guests to share the day with them. The travel company will even provide a professional best man and bridesmaid, suitably attired to complement the bridal couple and act as witnesses, or the couple may prefer to arrange witnesses among friends they have made while at the hotel. Even though it is hot and the ceremony takes place almost on the beach, most brides choose to wear a formal white wedding dress and grooms a lounge or morning suit, dinner jacket or white tuxedo.

All this sun, sea, sand and romance sounds wonderful, but to avoid disappointment the prospective bride and groom should think seriously, look at the pictures in depth and read the small print before deciding if this is really the kind of wedding for them.

PART TWO
Celebrating

7

RECEPTION VENUE

Before you can book the venue for the reception, you will have to decide what kind of celebration you want and in what kind of surroundings, and, most important, how much you can afford to spend! Do you want a grand hotel or restaurant setting, with chandeliers and wall to wall waiters carrying trays of champagne (expensive!), a country hotel with beautiful grounds (good for photographs), a marquee in the garden (more private and relaxed), a function room in the civic hall or local pub, or a simpler affair in the village hall or your own home, doing the catering yourself (hard work, but friendly and much cheaper)?

Try and find somewhere convenient, preferably not too far from the church or Register Office. Ask opinions of seemingly suitable venues among friends who have been involved in recent weddings, and *always visit any hotel, restaurant or hall before making a decision.* Don't rely on phone calls or pictures in brochures, which, like travel brochures, always show everything to their best advantage.

You will have to decide on the appropriate number of guests to be invited, as this dictates the size of room needed – there should be sufficient space for people to move about in comfort, but it should not be so large that the place feels half empty and everyone huddles at one end of a vast banqueting hall. A sit down meal needs more space than a buffet, although adequate seating should always be provided for guests to sit and chat, as weddings are great for catching up on news of family and friends, and there should be plenty of tables for plates and glasses.

You must also decide on the type of catering: whether to have a serious sit down dinner, a fork buffet or finger food. If the reception is not to be held in a hotel or restaurant, you will need to decide whether to hire caterers or do the food yourself. It must also be decided if there is to be an evening reception, at the same or a different venue, and the type of catering for that too. Drinks will also have to be provided, either by the hotel, caterer or yourselves, and perhaps music during the reception and later at the evening party, if appropriate.

Hotel, Restaurant, Club or Function Room
Popular venues for wedding receptions get booked up well in advance (12-18 months is quite common), particularly on Saturdays and Public Holidays, so if you've set your heart on a particular hotel it would be wise to make some tentative enquiries regarding availability before setting the wedding date. Even if you decide to get married just a few weeks or months ahead, it's still worth enquiring at your first venue choice as that particular date may still be free, or there may have been a last minute cancellation of a wedding booked months in advance. Go incognito and have a meal at any hotel or restaurant you are considering, and if you are pleased with the food then make enquiries about wedding receptions.

There is often a functions manager or wedding consultant who will send you a brochure outlining what the hotel has to offer, and then arrange an appointment for you to visit and see the rooms available and discuss all aspects of the reception: number of guests, size of rooms, type of meal and suggested menus, drinks, arrangements for receiving the guests as they arrive, type of tables and seating arrangements, waiting staff, toastmaster or Master of Ceremonies if appropriate, floral decorations, band or other music, changing room for bride and groom, overnight accommodation for the couple and/or guests if required (this may be part of a wedding package offered by the hotel, often with complementary bridal suite and special rates for the guests). If there is not to be an evening party at the hotel, check for how long the room will be available and whether everyone will have to leave by a certain time.

If it is a large hotel or restaurant, ask about arrangements for the other guests who may be staying there, and check if your party will have a private reception area or will be sharing the bar with other visitors. Look at the cloakroom facilities. (I was once at a large hotel where a wedding reception was in full swing and on visiting the ladies room I was confronted by a giggling bride who was attempting to 'visit the bathroom' while three long-skirted bridesmaids tried to lift her voluminous wedding dress clear of the damp, none-too-pristine tiled cloakroom floor!)

Once you have booked the reception, the manager or wedding consultant should take over all the responsibility for the day, while remaining in close consultation with the bride and her mother (or whoever is organising the wedding). He or she should be able to advise you on menus in detail, giving you several sample menus to study and then adapting them to suit your personal preferences, or to include the bride and groom's favourite dishes (ours had to include the groom's favourite chocolate roulade). You will need to discuss your drink require-ments with the hotel at the same time (see page 61).

Discuss all other personal arrangements you want well in advance – floral and table decorations to match the bridal bouquet, table linen to complement the colour scheme, seating plans (long or round tables) and place cards (whether you or the hotel will write them). Talk about music if it is to be provided, and check arrangements for setting up and displaying the wedding cake, whether it is to be provided by the hotel or supplied by a professional decorator or yourself. Also, arrange for the display of the wedding presents if you wish.

Marquees at Hotels
Occasionally a hotel with a suitable garden may suggest holding the reception in a marquee in the grounds, if they have no suitable function room or the wedding party wants to go on longer than the hotel would have room inside available. The hotel would supply and furnish the marquee and provide the reception as if it was taking place within the main house.

Marquees at Home
If you have a large enough garden (and it's amazing how a marquee will fit into a seemingly small space) this can be the ideal solution to holding the reception at home. The inside of the marquee can look most elegant and inviting, with a lining, built-in floor and pretty floral decorations, while on a lovely summer's day the sides can be rolled up to let in the sunshine, and if you employ professional caterers it should be no more work for the bride and her mother than going to a hotel.

However, it is not a cheap option: by the time you've paid for the marquee with all the extra fixtures and fittings (lining, flooring, dance floor, lighting, windows, tables, chairs and heating in the winter), plus the cost of floral decor and the catering, the price will be similar to, or more expensive than, that of a hotel. The benefits are that the atmosphere will be much more personal and everything will be more convenient. The bride and groom will have everything to hand when they go to change to go away, and any young children can be safely put to bed on the premises with a baby alarm plugged in or Grandma resting downstairs during the evening reception.

Before deciding to hold the reception in a marquee at home, give some thought to the practicalities involved. Are you able, and happy, to spend hours tidying the garden and arranging (or borrowing) tubs and urns to decorate the surrounds? (You may need to start preparations months ahead if the bride is to be greeted by her favourite flowers on arrival back from the ceremony.) You will have to decide if the guests are to make use of the house or if they will enter the marquee directly from the road or the garden, and you will need to make arrangements for adequate toilet facilities. For a very big occasion portaloos can be hired, either through the marquee company or the caterers, but generally the guests use the toilets and bathrooms in the house, provided they are clearly marked and easily accessible from the marquee. (Paper towels and waste paper baskets in the bathroom save guests being confronted by wet hand towels.) Make sure there are plenty of spare loo rolls too!

Marquee companies can be found from Yellow Pages or adverts in the local press, and some catering companies will provide a marquee if required. The company will send you a brochure of photographs and a comprehensive price list (prices vary according to type of tent, either a traditional marquee with tent poles and ropes, or a free-standing frame tent), including the cost of all the extra necessities and accessories. They will send a representative to advise you on the most suitable marquee for your site, and estimate the size needed to accommodate the number of guests for the type of meal chosen, help with choosing size and type of tables (round or long trestles), types of chairs (from plastic garden chairs to upholstered banquet chairs), and advise on the basic layout of the marquee for the type of meal to be served. They will have samples of different coloured linings and types of flooring or matting available, advise on size of dance floor needed if appropriate, types of lighting (chandeliers, wall lights and/or spots), windows and French doors if you wish, and an adjoining catering tent and serving tables for the caterers' use if the food is not being prepared in your kitchen.

Professional caterers usually bring their own stoves and equipment if a hot meal is being served, and will prepare this in the catering tent out of sight of the guests. The marquee company will need to run an electric cable from the house for the lights and the caterer may need an electricity supply for cooking and heating equipment. The company will supply the cable but will need to know where they can safely and unobtrusively plug it in, without danger of staff or guests tripping over.

Always choose a marquee company who actually visit the site, as they will then be aware of any problems regarding access or erecting the marquee (they may need to avoid your special flower bed or fit it in between a group of trees). *Do not* employ a company who just send a brochure and quote over the phone.

The company will ask for a deposit when you make the booking, with the final bill being settled when the marquee is erected – usually 2-3 days before the wedding, thus giving you and the caterers time to make any last minute arrangements, put up the floral decorations and to use the marquee, as we did, to entertain guests the night before. Our bride's family and friends arrived from Germany the morning before the wedding (travelling en masse in a fleet of hired cars and a minibus from Heathrow), and stayed in B&Bs and neighbours' houses around the village, as did most of the groom's family and friends who travelled from around the country to attend. In order to feed everyone we had a pre-wedding party in the marquee, with enormous trays of home-made lasagne, big bowls of salad, hot bread rolls and butter, followed by a selection of choc ices (in paper to save washing up), all washed down with plenty of wine. By the end of the evening both 'sides' knew each other, and it was a lovely start to the wedding weekend.

Civic, Church or Village Hall

A less expensive option could be to hire a hall for the day, and either do the catering yourself with plenty of help from family and friends, or to hire a caterer to prepare and serve the food. Go and look at the hall and surroundings before booking – some halls are most attractive and welcoming, while others are used mainly for jumble sales and indoor sports and may look a bit run down or even in need of a good clean before you'd want to use them for a wedding reception. Check kitchen and toilet facilities, provision of floral decor (if any), and availability of tables, chairs, linen, glasses, china and cutlery (and if they are of a suitable standard to use at the reception). If it is a winter wedding, make sure there will be adequate heating. Check how long you will have use of the hall; you'll need time beforehand to get everything ready, and you don't want to find the badminton club or a keep fit class waiting to use the hall while the bride and groom are still getting round to cutting the cake.

If you are doing the catering yourself, make sure there will be some help available to sort out the tables and chairs and lift down heavy boxes of china. Check that everything will be washed and ready to use on the day, not just taken out of a dusty cupboard, or that you can do this yourself in advance if necessary. Look at the cooking facilities if you are going to serve any hot dishes, and make sure you know how to work the urns for tea and coffee making (and how many cups they hold), or make sure there are sufficient kettles for your needs. Check refrigeration space for foods – meat and fish dishes, salads and creamy desserts must not be left waiting in a warm room for hours before being served – and you'll need somewhere to keep the wine and beer cold (a clean dustbin filled with ice is a good option). Make sure there is also some space in the kitchen to set out, garnish and decorate the food, although it will probably be easier to cook and prepare everything at home, doing the minimum of preparation at the hall.

Make arrangements about clearing up afterwards: decide who will be responsible for the washing up and putting away (neither the bride's mother nor the groom's mother will feel like doing it late in the evening after the bride and groom have left, and the bride will have a watertight excuse for escaping the washing up). Someone will also need to be responsible for locking up the hall when everyone has gone.

If you are hiring caterers to do the food, they will need to inspect the premises themselves to check what equipment they need to bring with them. You should also establish if the caterers provide the china, glasses, linen etc., or whether you need to hire that from the hall or elsewhere.

At Home
A very small, informal reception can be lovely when held at home, provided you can arrange your sitting and dining rooms to

accommodate comfortably the number of guests invited – and numbers soon mount up even with just family from both sides and a few close friends. Because of the convenience this is a popular choice for the reception venue at the marriage of an older widowed or divorced couple, where the catering may be provided by the bride or groom's grown up children. It is also a popular choice with couples who have been living together for a while and want a simple celebration in their own home.

Try and do as much in advance as possible. Collect china, glasses, cutlery and table linen which you may need to borrow from neighbours or friends. Glasses are often available on free loan from the off licence or wine merchant, and you can usually buy the wine and beer on a sale or return basis. Decide if you need to borrow extra serving dishes and if you will need extra kettles for the numerous cups of tea and coffee. If necessary, everything can be hired from specialist hire companies, which can be found in Yellow Pages. Find the bottle opener or corkscrew, and make arrangements to keep champagne, wine, beers and soft drinks cold. A clean dustbin filled with (bought) ice is a good option, unless you have plenty of refrigerator space or can borrow room in your neighbours' fridges. Decide on the type of menu (buffet or sit down meal) and do as much of the preparation as possible well in advance, freezing as many dishes as you can, ready to defrost overnight or on the day.

The day before the wedding have a thorough clean through the house, just leaving a quick hoover and tidy and a swift wipe of the bathroom in the morning. Arrange the flowers for the house and table, and if possible set the table and put out china, glasses and serving dishes and arrange the furniture, leaving as little as possible to see to before setting off for the church or Register Office.

Try and enlist as much help as you can with final preparation and serving of the food on the day, to ensure that the bride, and her mother or daughter, also have time to relax and enjoy themselves. Alternatively, consider hiring caterers to provide the food and drinks in your own home, so that you can arrive back from the service to find everything ready and waiting.

8

CATERING

Professional Caterers at Home or Hall
Choosing a caterer can be difficult. You can find plenty of
names through adverts in the local press, at Wedding Fayres or
in Yellow Pages, of firms who will be delighted to send you
ideas and sample menus, but it is essential to meet them
personally to discuss exactly what they are able to provide and
how they will manage the cooking and serving of the meal in
the marquee, hall or your own home. It is best to try and sample
their work or to get a personal recommendation from friends
who have attended one of their functions.

Once you have decided on the type of menu (finger food, fork
buffet or sit down dinner), the caterer will need to visit the
house or hall with you to decide what equipment will be
required and who will provide it. For a small reception or cold
buffet, the caterer may be able to manage just using your
kitchen, bringing the food ready cooked, leaving a minimum of
reheating and just tea and coffee making, but for a large
reception hot meal they will need to bring a catering size
cooker, hot water urns and extra refrigeration for food and
wines. (For our August wedding our caterer brought a refriger-
ated van, rather like a small horse box, which was set up 24
hours in advance, to chill the drinks and provide plenty of room
to keep the food and finished dishes cool before serving.) The
caterer will also need some kitchen and serving tables, generally
supplied by the marquee company or the hall, but the caterer
can usually provide china, glasses and table linen if necessary.

Discuss the provision of waiting staff, the method of serving
drinks and the meal, and whether the head waiter will act as
MC/toastmaster if you wish. Most caterers will be delighted to
provide the drinks, or you may prefer to buy these yourself,

leaving the caterer to open the bottles and serve the drinks, but check if there will be any extra charge for this. Decide how long you want the waiting staff to stay on after the meal, and if you need waiters to serve tea, coffee, soft and alcoholic drinks until the guests are ready to leave or if you will make arrangements for people to help themselves.

If there is to be an evening reception decide if there is to be a gap in between when the staff can take a break and have time to clear and possibly rearrange the room for dancing, and set out the evening buffet. Make arrangements for clearing away at the end of the reception (if you are hiring a hall this may need to be completed before leaving that evening), and make arrangements for collecting and removing all the catering equipment, probably next day or on a Monday morning after a Saturday wedding.

Catering Yourself
The bride or her mother (or anyone else!) needs to think very carefully before deciding to do the catering for the reception personally, either at home or in a hall. The bride will be busy enough on her wedding morning (hairdresser, make up, wedding dress, last minute nerves), without having to spend hours in the kitchen, and the bride's mother will want to enjoy the day too, and be with the guests at the reception.

If you do decide on DIY, choose your menu carefully, bearing in mind you want to do the minimum possible on the day. Prepare as much as you can well in advance, freezing dishes which will be ready to serve once defrosted, without any further work. (Don't defrost them too early or they'll take up space in the fridge!) A wide variety of frozen foods and finished frozen dishes, ready to defrost and cook if necessary, are available from supermarkets (lots of different canapés, quiches, pies, vol au vents, main course dishes and deliciously wicked desserts). All kinds of freshly cooked, decorated ready-to-serve foods and finished dishes are also available from supermarkets and delicatessens, either over the counter or to order. Specialist caterers will supply fresh, ready-cooked dishes as well which can be mixed and matched with your own home cooked food. These can be collected or delivered the day before (if suitable) or early on the wedding morning.

When catering for a large number of people it is particularly important to prepare food hygienically, and to store it safely for as short a time as possible before it is eaten. Fresh or defrosted ingredients and finished dishes must be kept covered and stored in the fridge if appropriate, and should not be set out on the serving tables in a warm room for hours before the guests arrive.

Empty your fridge of all unnecessary items in order to provide as much space as possible for the wedding food (or even buy a secondhand fridge and/or freezer, often available very cheaply through post card adverts in the paper shop, to use for the wedding and then resell), and make sure that 'someone' does not commandeer all the fridge space to chill the wine and beer! You may be able to borrow refrigerator and freezer space from neighbours, and will probably have to keep the drinks cold in a bin of supermarket ice.

Check that you have enough china, cutlery, serving dishes, glasses and table linen – you may need to borrow from neighbours or hire extra items (see Yellow Pages), while glasses are often loaned free of charge from the off licence when you buy the drinks, and pretty paper table linen is widely available. Although paper plates are sometimes a bit flimsy they do save an awful lot of work!

If possible, set up the reception room the day before, arranging the flowers and table decorations, setting the tables, putting out china, cutlery, napkins and glasses, and setting up the bar. Don't forget the table to display the wedding cake. If the reception is in a hall, decide in advance how you are going to transport all the food and drink to the hall on the wedding morning, and make sure you have plenty of help setting it out.

Try and recruit 'someone' (friend, relative or neighbour) who will either stay at home or at the hall, or slip away early from the service in order to uncover the food and set it ready on the tables. This 'someone' can then also pour the drinks to greet bride, groom and guests as they arrive for the reception.

The Food

Finger Buffet

This can vary from a very simple affair, with a glass of wine, crisps and salted nuts, to a full meal with assorted canapés, dips, sandwiches, filled or open rolls, filo pastry savouries, sausage rolls, vol au vents, chicken satay, battered prawns and vegetables etc. served hot or cold, followed by tiny meringues, eclairs and other desserts that can be eaten without a fork. The buffet can be set out on a table for guests to help themselves, or brought round by waiting staff. This type of menu, although it sounds simple, requires a lot of last minute preparation and assembly on the day, so it may be more suitable for professional caterers, unless the bride, or her mother, has plenty of competent, reliable helpers. Although the guests will stand or 'circulate' on arrival, ensure that there are sufficient chairs and tables for people to sit down as the reception proceeds. Space will be needed on the buffet table for the wedding cake, or it can be displayed on a separate table. Make arrangements to greet your guests as they arrive from the service, usually with a glass of wine or sherry, champagne, sparkling wine or Buck's Fizz, or a soft drink, offered to them when they have passed along the formal receiving line (see page 68).

Fork Buffet
This can be a cold meal, with cooked meats and fish, quiches, pies and lots of 'interesting' salads, or can include some more substantial hot dishes – casseroles, curries and spicy dishes, pastry dishes and vegetarian specials, or a 'carvery' with roast meat or poultry, hot vegetables and sauces – followed by hot and/or cold puddings and desserts. For those catering for a DIY reception, a fork buffet menu has the big advantage that most of the dishes can be prepared beforehand and stored in the freezer, and much of the salad and vegetable preparation can be done the day before, leaving a minimum of defrosting, decorating and last minute preparation on the day. You may need to borrow space in neighbours' freezers and make use of their ovens for last-minute reheating. The tables can be arranged as for a sit down meal, with seating plan and place cards, ready set with china, cutlery, glasses and napkins. Bread rolls, butter, bowls of salad and bottles of wine can be placed on the tables, just leaving the guests to help themselves to main courses from the buffet table, or you can be more informal, leaving people to help themselves completely from the buffet table, collecting napkin, cutlery and glass of wine before sitting down to eat. Make sure there are sufficient tables and chairs for everyone; it's difficult

trying to eat with a fork, butter a bread roll and balance a glass of wine while standing up! The wedding cake can be placed as a centre piece on the buffet table or displayed on a small table nearby.

Professional caterers will make provision for serving the food and clearing away used plates and glasses, but if you are doing the food yourself it would be sensible for 'someone' to help with the serving and clearing up, so that the wedding party can all be free to enjoy the occasion with the guests. Make arrangements for greeting the guests and serving arrival drinks as for a sit down meal (see page 68).

Hot or Cold Sit Down Dinner
Unless you have an enormous amount of help from friends and neighbours, or a *very* small wedding party, this is definitely an option for hotel, restaurant or professional caterers. The hotel or caterer will discuss sample menus, and help you choose the meal and method of serving it – plated meals with or without separate dishes of vegetables on the tables, or silver service throughout. Some hotels offer a choice of dishes for each course, but they may need to have the numbers for each choice in advance (which can get very complicated), while other menus just include a vegetarian option and perhaps a choice of puds. When deciding your menu, let the caterer know of any special dietary needs and the number of vegetarians amongst your guests.

You will need to discuss the type of seating arrangements (long or round tables), and the size of the 'top table' for the wedding party. When arranging the tables, remember that a long top table only seats the wedding party on one side so that they are facing the guests, and, as at any dinner party, a great deal of thought will have to be given in regard to the seating of the guests, whether to mix 'both sides' or keep the families separate, and to make sure there will be no feuds between neighbours. You will also need to draw up a seating plan to be displayed near the entrance to the dining room (see page 69), and decide who will supply and write the place cards (you or the caterer).

Drinks
Whatever kind of meal or menu you are providing, drinks at a wedding reception usually follow the same pattern: drink(s) on

arrival (sherry, red or white wine, sparkling wine, champagne, Buck's Fizz or fruit juice), usually a selection ready-poured to be offered to the guests as they enter the room or reach the end of the receiving line, with other soft drinks and beers available on request. Red wine is not so popular at weddings, and often only white wine is offered. Buck's Fizz will cut down the cost of sparkling wine or champagne, while giving a festive feeling to the occasion. Table wines are usually served with the meal, and sparkling wine or champagne for the toasts. You may choose to serve simply red or white 'house' wines, or select different wines for each course, including a dessert wine and liqueurs, or to serve champagne throughout the reception. *Decide in advance with the hotel, restaurant or caterer exactly what drinks are to be made available at your expense, and when, or if, the guests will have to start buying their own alcoholic beverages.*

Many hotels now offer a drinks package, priced at so much per guest, usually including a welcome drink, 1 or 2 glasses of wine with the meal and 1 or 2 glasses of sparkling wine or champagne for the toasts, or you may prefer to agree a certain number of bottles of wine to be placed on the tables and allow the guests to help themselves. Most people like to provide beers and lagers as well as soft drinks as an alternative to wines – depending on your guests this may or may not be a cheaper option! Decide if there is to be a bar available to the guests for those who want bar drinks (spirits, mixers, beers, lagers etc.), and if it is to be a free bar (i.e. paid for by you – could be very expensive!) or if your guests must buy their own extra drinks.

If you wish to provide the bottles of drinks yourself, possibly bringing champagne, wines and beers back from the Continent, you will have to negotiate with the hotel or restaurant regarding corkage and serving. Many hotels charge quite a hefty amount per bottle if you provide your own wines, but caterers are usually more willing to provide this service free of extra charge, but they will need to have the bottles in plenty of time to get them chilled before serving. If you are providing the drinks yourself, at home or in a marquee particularly, the main worry is how much people are going to drink and whether you will run out of anything. If you are bringing the drink home from abroad you will have to rely on an approximate calculation, erring on the generous side, but if you are buying from a wine merchant, off licence or supermarket, there may be a 'sale or return' option available, and the free 'hire' of glasses which can be useful if you are doing the catering in a hall or at home.

Estimating how much drink you will need

Sherry   — allow 1-2 glasses per person
              1 litre bottle   = 12-16 glasses
              1 x 75cl. bottle   = 8-10 glasses

Table Wine — allow 2-3 glasses/$^1/_2$ bottle per person
                                             (or more!)
              1 litre bottle   = 8-9 glasses
              1 x 75cl. bottle   = 6-7 glasses

Champagne or Sparkling Wine –
              allow 1-2 glasses per person (or more!)
              1 litre bottle   = 8-10 glasses
              1 x 75cl. bottle   = 6-8 glasses

Squash, Fruit Juice, Bottled Water –
              1 litre bottle squash   = 30-40 glasses
                                          when diluted
              1 litre pack / fruit juice = 6-8 glasses
              1 litre bottle water   = 5-6 glasses

Beers and Lagers

These can be bought by the crate or pack. You'll know your guests and will have to decide how much you're likely to need!

Don't forget to stock up on mixers – tonic, dry ginger, bitter lemon, etc. – if you are going to serve any spirits (the litre bottles are cheaper than individual ones) and get in plenty of cans of coke or other soft drinks, and bottles of 'designer' water to place on the tables. If the reception is in an unlicensed hall, marquee or your own home, don't forget it is unlawful to sell alcohol without a licence.

9

THE WEDDING CAKE

A beautiful wedding cake is a very special part of a traditional wedding reception. The rich, heavy cake is supposed to symbolise fertility and bring happiness to the bride and groom and good luck to everyone who tastes a piece.

The cake can be provided by the hotel or caterers as part of the reception, or you can order a cake from a professional bakery and have it delivered to the wedding reception venue on the day. Another option is to bake the cake at home and then have it professionally iced (as I did), or, if you have the time and expertise, you can bake and ice the cake yourself. Cake tins can be hired from specialist cake shops, or a private cake decorator may have tins that she is willing to lend you.

Wedding cakes can be one, two, three or more tiers high (two or three being the most usual), depending on the number of guests at the reception and the number of people unable to attend to whom you want to give some cake. If one of the families comes from a distance away, the relevant mother may want to take one of the smaller tiers or a chunk of the big tier to distribute to family and friends who have not travelled to the wedding. Sometimes the top tier is kept by the bride and groom to use in the future at the christening of their first child, or cut on their first anniversary.

Traditionally the wedding cake was square, round or lucky horseshoe shaped, made from a rich fruit cake base, covered with marzipan and white royal icing (which sometimes went very hard!), beautifully decorated with white or pastel icing scrolls and flowers, and dotted about with little wedding rings, love birds, lucky slippers and 'silver' horseshoes. Each tier could be tied round with white ribbon or a silver paper frill.

Nowadays a softer, easier to cut moulding or fondant icing is often used, although the traditional royal icing is still preferred by some couples. The top tier, or a single tier cake, can be a sponge or chocolate cake if you don't like fruit cake, but I'd be wary of a three-tier sponge cake: it might collapse under the weight!

A professional baker or cake decorator will have lots of ideas to help you choose your wedding cake. You may want the cake to match the wedding dress and bouquets, or to incorporate a particular personal design relating to the bride and groom's professions or interests – university or school colours, service badges or club emblems, for example.

If your hotel or caterer is not making the cake, enquire at your local baker or specialist cake shop. Even if they don't make and ice wedding cakes themselves they may be able to supply the names and phone numbers of other shops, or perhaps they display a list of people who do. There are also cake decorating shops, some of whom decorate birthday, celebration and wedding cakes in public view, and others that sell or hire everything necessary for decorating all kinds of special occasion cakes, from cake tins to cake stands, icing tubes, silver ribbon and cake decorations, and they will almost certainly have a list of people who will make and/or ice and decorate cakes to special order. This was how we found Eileen, who decorated our cake, and who we later discovered had been at school with the bridegroom.

There are lots of books on cake decorating available in bookshops and libraries to give more ideas, some of which are very traditional, some very modern and some quite outrageous. A professional decorator should also have a book of pictures of cake designs, and, usually, photos of cakes that she has made previously to help you decide. When we were choosing our cake we studied the album of photos the decorator lent us showing 'her' cakes, and added our own ideas, to design between us a lovely ivory coloured three-tier cake, decorated with tiny fondant rosebuds and ivy leaves to match the wedding bouquet, each tier topped with a spray of exquisite fondant roses. The whole effect was quite stunning.

The traditional cake is topped with a small silver vase holding a few fresh flowers to match the bridal bouquet, or a small spray of flowers can be laid on the top (these should be ordered with the bouquets and arrangements made for them to be sent with the other flowers or collected by the caterers). If you don't want to use fresh flowers, a spray of spun sugar flowers or flowers made from fondant icing that match the bouquet (as we chose) look most effective. These are easily made by a professional, but may take a little practice if you are inexperienced at making them yourself. A further choice that many people prefer are any number of 'Wedding Cake Decorations' available from specialist cake shops and many stationers – plastic bride and grooms, lucky horseshoes, teddies dressed in wedding finery, decorated wedding cars and carriages. The choice is vast.

The cakes should be made 2-3 months in advance if possible, to give them time to mature, but they should not be marzipanned, iced and decorated until nearer the time, to ensure that the icing does not discolour. For the traditional tiered cake, each tier must be in proportion in width, depth and height to give the desired effect (although you can cheat a bit with extra marzipan padding under the icing if necessary). Allow 7.5cm (3") between sizes of each tier to give a stable, well proportioned cake. The horseshoe cake is most effective if only one or at most two tiers high, as further tiers become very small and narrow.

If you are baking the cakes yourself, to ensure a good deep, solid cake (important if you are supporting several tiers one above the other), cheat and make the next size cake recipe but bake it in the smaller tin (i.e. 22.5cm (9") square amount baked in a 20cm (8") square tin). See the Appendix for a chart showing the approximate number of pieces you can expect to get out of square, round or horseshoe cakes of various sizes.

The finished tiers are erected on cake pillars which either balance on top of royal iced cakes or can be secured into fondant icing with special little plastic rods. These pillars are available from specialist cake shops. Each tier usually stands on a 'silver' board, which can be iced and decorated if liked, and then the whole cake is set up on a special stand, ideally on a small table in a convenient place, ready to be cut ceremoniously by bride and groom together.

Check with the caterers about setting up the finished cake before the reception. Traditionally the cake is placed on a 'silver' stand and cut with a decorative 'silver' knife, and this is usually included in the cost of the cake or decorations. The cake can be cut with a sword if there are family connections with the services, but you will have to supply your own weapon.

Do make sure that the cake is set up in a safe place, perhaps as part of the buffet table, or on a separate table well away from the main area through which guests or waiters will be walking – not where it could be carelessly knocked by a passing waiter. Also check, especially if the reception is in a marquee, that the table is level and that the floor around it doesn't 'bounce' when people walk past. I have heard a story (vouched for by our Master of Ceremonies) of a three-tier cake that slowly slid sideways just before the wedding party returned from the church! The table can be decorated with a pretty cloth and the bridal bouquets.

Prices of cakes, icing and decorating will vary according to the size of cake and amount of decoration. Check exactly what you are being offered, as, again, the most expensive may not necessarily be the best. Large commercial bakeries should produce a good quality cake, probably to a set design, whereas a small company or private decorator will be able to give a more personal service. The choice is yours, and I hope that you will be as pleased with your cake as we were with ours.

10

RECEIVING, SEATING, SPEECHES & BEYOND

Whatever type of meal is being served, draw up a rough timetable for 'The Day' (see Appendix) to ensure the food is ready when guests arrive. Allow time for the ceremony, photographs afterwards and travel from ceremony to reception (unless it's a civil wedding with ceremony and reception at one venue). Ensure the caterer has access to hall or marquee the day before or early on the wedding day, as required, to set up catering equipment, arrange and set tables, set up the bar and prepare the food and drinks ready to serve as guests arrive.

Greeting Guests

Many couples like to greet their guests with a formal receiving line near the entrance, or it may be more convenient for guests to come into the reception area, leave their coats if necessary and then 'mingle', with drinks, until the meal is served. The receiving line can then form and guests pass along the line as they proceed into the dining room to take their places.

Receiving Line

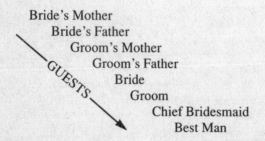

Bride's Mother
Bride's Father
Groom's Mother
Groom's Father
GUESTS
Bride
Groom
Chief Bridesmaid
Best Man

If there is to be a formal meal, the wedding party take their places at the top table when all the guests are seated. The bridal party, led by the bride and groom, followed by the bride's father with the groom's mother, the groom's father with the bride's mother, the best man with the chief bridesmaid and the ushers with the other bridesmaids, make their way to the top table, possibly amidst applause from the guests. If there is no formal seating plan for a buffet meal, the wedding party mingle with their guests, although sometimes a 'Top Table' is still reserved for the bridal party.

Seating Plan
This can be as formal or casual as you wish. The bride and groom sit at the centre of the top table, with both sets of parents, the best man and chief bridesmaid. According to the size of the table, other bridesmaids and ushers may also sit there or may be seated amongst other guests. The immediate family and closest friends sit nearest to the top table, with other relatives and friends sitting farther away. It is up to you whether you mix the 'two sides' or seat them at separate tables!

Husbands and wives, girl and boy friends are usually seated near together, and small children should be with their parents. It is nice to put friends who may not have met for a while together – perhaps old school or college friends of bride and groom – but care must be taken that no-one feels left out, or is the only one seated at a table where everyone else are old friends.

Make sure that the caterer will provide adequate waiting staff to serve a sit down meal to all the tables at approximately the same time, so that there are no embarrassing pauses when one table has finished eating while others are still waiting to be served. If you're having a 'serve yourself' buffet, try and have at least two sets of food on the table, so that guests can form two queues instead of one very long line, and at a formal buffet, a waiter can invite one or two tables at a time to help themselves. At all types of meal, the top table is always served first.

Check beforehand whether the head waiter will act as MC or toastmaster if you wish, and make sure that he has a list of the names of those who will give the speeches. If there is a member of the clergy present, it is usual to ask him or her to say grace before the meal.

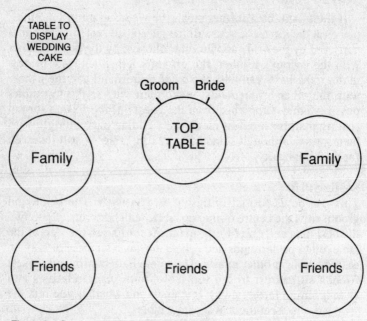

Figure 3a: Seating plan for round tables

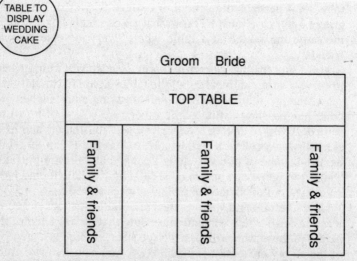

Figure 3b: Seating plan for straight tables

1. Chief Bridesmaid
   Groom's Father
   Bride's Mother
   Bridegroom
   Bride
   Bride's Father
   Groom's Mother
   Best Man

2. Usher
   Chief Bridesmaid
   Groom's Father
   Bride's Mother
   Bridegroom
   Bride
   Bride's Father
   Groom's Mother
   Best Man
   Bridesmaid

3. Groom's Mother
   Bride's Father
   Chief Bridesmaid
   Bridegroom
   Bride
   Best Man
   Bride's Mother
   Groom's Father

4. Usher
   Chief Bridesmaid
   Bride's Father
   Bride's Mother
   Bridegroom
   Bride
   Groom's Father
   Groom's Mother
   Best Man
   Bridesmaid

Figure 3c: Alternative seating orders for the Top Table

Cutting the Cake
The ceremony of cutting the cake may take place after the best man's speech (or at the end of any extra speeches), or it can take place before the speeches begin. The bride and groom will just make a token cut with the ceremonial knife into the bottom tier of the cake which is then removed by the caterer and sliced ready for distribution. Having the ceremonial cutting before the speeches means that the caterers can have the cake ready for distribution as soon as the speeches finish. The cake can be handed out by the bridesmaids (younger ones will enjoy this 'important' job), or by the waiters.

Speeches

Traditionally only three speeches are made at the reception, but nowadays the bride, chief bridesmaid and other family members or close friends may also choose to say a few words. If there is no official toastmaster or Master of Ceremonies provided by the caterer, the best man usually undertakes these duties.

The bride's father, or other male relative of the bride (usually whoever has given her away), proposes a toast to the health and happiness of the bride and groom. If the bride's father is unable to make this speech, the task should be delegated well in advance, so that whoever is making the speech is not taken unawares at the last minute. The speech should be quite short, and usually welcomes the guests and thanks them for attending the wedding, and then welcomes the new son-in-law into the family, making the oft heard reference to gaining a son, not losing a daughter. The bridegroom's parents are also mentioned, and often a reference to the happiness the bride has brought to her own parents during her life with them. A few words of advice for the couple's married life together may also be included, before proposing 'A toast to the Health and Happiness of the bride and groom'.

The bridegroom replies on behalf of his wife and himself (usually beginning 'my wife and I' for the first time in his married life), thanking everyone for their good wishes and wonderful presents. He thanks his own parents for their care and attention to him in the past, and for any particular sacrifices they have made on his behalf, and thanks the bride's parents for all they have done to provide such a lovely wedding and splendid reception, and for allowing him to marry their beautiful daughter, to whom he intends to devote the rest of his life in pursuit of her happiness. He thanks everyone who has helped in any capacity to make the wedding ceremony and reception such a success, and thanks the best man for his assistance (or otherwise) in the preparation for the wedding, and lastly thanks the bridesmaids for looking so lovely and for all their help before and during the service. The speech concludes with a toast to 'The Bridesmaids'.

(It is traditional, but not compulsory, for the bride and groom to thank the bridesmaids, pageboys, best man and ushers for all their help and hard work with a small gift. These may be distributed before everyone leaves for the ceremony, sometime during the day, or, as is often the case, during the groom's speech as he thanks each in turn. It is nice to choose something which can be kept as a memento: often jewellery (but *not* rings as the bride is the one with the ring on the wedding day!) or a photoframe for the bridesmaids; engraved tankards, tie clips, cufflinks or a bottle of something for ushers and best man. It is also a nice gesture to surprise both the 'mothers of' with bouquets of flowers or lovely pot plants as a sign of appreciation for all their hard work. Traditionally the groom paid for these gifts, but now the bride usually shares the cost.)

The best man responds on behalf of the bridesmaids, usually with a light-hearted speech containing references to the bridegroom's luck in finding such a lovely bride, and amazement that she should have made such a poor choice of husband when she could have taken her pick of all the groom's jealous friends! He may include some episodes concerning the bridegroom in his bachelor days (as long as they will not embarrass or otherwise upset the bride). He thanks the groom for his good wishes to the bridesmaids, and concludes by wishing the couple good luck in their life together.

After this the best man reads out any telemessages that British Telecom have actually managed to deliver on time (having first checked that they are suitable to read out at a family gathering), and may also read out cards of good wishes received by the couple from friends unable to attend the wedding. The cards and messages should be given to the bride's mother for safekeeping with the wedding presents until the bride returns from her honeymoon.

Displaying the Wedding Presents

Everyone will be interested to see the gifts received by the couple, and these are often set out on a convenient table at the reception so that the guests can admire them at their leisure. Presents received before the wedding day should be opened and set out on the table before the reception, while presents brought along on the day can be displayed in their pretty wrappings, and if there is time they can be opened by the couple during the reception. The display should be made to look as attractive as possible, and the gift cards should be attached to or displayed next to each gift. (It is wise to make a list of who sent what, in case the cards get moved about.) A list of people who have sent gifts of money, cheques, shares etc. should be displayed (but not the actual cheque or certificates), although the value or amounts should not be disclosed. 'Someone' will have to arrange to transport the gifts to the reception and it may be more convenient to do this a day or two before the wedding and arrangements made to set them out in the reception room; a good hotel or caterer may be able to set up the display for you as long as this is discussed in advance. (Do make sure, however, that good security arrangements are in force to prevent theft/damage.) 'Someone' will also have to be responsible for getting the gifts safely back to the bride's parents' house or to the couple's home.

If it is not convenient to display the gifts at the reception, they can be displayed at the home of the bride's parents or at the couple's own home, and wedding guests, friends and neighbours invited to view them after the wedding.

Thank-you letters for all the gifts, however small, must of course be sent out by bride and groom as soon as possible, either before the wedding or on return from the honeymoon.

Evening Reception
You will have to decide if the afternoon reception is to carry on into the evening at the same venue, with all the guests remaining, possibly with extra guests invited to come for the evening, or if the 'evening do' is to be a separate affair, with a different guest list, either at the same or a different venue. Often today, the afternoon reception is mostly for family, relatives and older friends, who have attended the marriage ceremony, while the evening party is for younger friends and colleagues of the bride and groom, enlivened with a group, band or disco. If the same guests are staying on and have already enjoyed a large meal in the afternoon, just light refreshments (crisps, nuts and some savouries) may be sufficient, but if another party of guests, particularly young people with hearty appetites, is invited, a more substantial buffet will be appreciated. It is most usual for the food to be set out on the buffet table and the guests invited to help themselves. The remaining complete tiers of the wedding cake may be left on display, and the bride and groom can cut the next tier for a different set of guests if they wish.

There are no set rules for drinks at the 'evening do'. At a hotel or restaurant the hosts may pay for a welcome arrival drink as at the afternoon reception, and then arrange for a bar to be made available at which the guests pay for their own drinks. This is common practice, especially when there are a lot of young people at the party, but the host may still prefer to pay for everything. If the reception is in an unlicensed hall, marquee or at home, you will not be able to sell drinks without a licence, so you will need to decide how much alcohol to provide or ask the guests to bring their own.

Our bride wanted a 'typical English day', and so, as most of the guests had already partaken of a hot three course meal with lots of wines in the afternoon, we decided on refreshing jugs of Pimms to be served in the evening (with beers, lagers and soft drinks as well), and large platters of assorted 'English' sandwiches, including smoked salmon, cucumber, egg and cress and the inevitable ham, to be placed on the tables at the evening 'do'.

Make sure there are sufficient tables and chairs for everyone, including, if possible, some quieter seats away from the disco or dance floor! If the guests are mostly young people it is sensible to ensure that there are a few older people there, generally the 'parents of' and a few of their friends, to keep an eye on things and make sure the couple get away safely at the end of the party.

Music at the Reception

The presence of music during the reception is one of personal taste – some people enjoy wall to wall musak, others can't stand it at any price. Check with the hotel or restaurant what, if anything, is normally provided. You may like some background music on tape or prefer to arrange for something completely different, perhaps a pianist, harpist or quiet group during the afternoon reception, with louder and more lively music (band and/or disco) in the evening. Make arrangements with the hotel or marquee company to provide a dance floor if you intend to dance.

It is wise to make enquiries about bands and discos as early as possible, as popular groups and good discos will get booked up well in advance. It may (or may not!) be best to let the bride and groom arrange the music, as younger people usually have a different taste in music from that of their parents! If the evening reception is mainly for younger people, this will cause no problems, but if it is for friends and relations of all ages, try and find something 'middle of the road' which everyone can enjoy. You can find musicians through local pubs, clubs and jazz clubs, adverts for concerts in the local press, recommendation by word of mouth ('someone' always knows of a good group!), or if all else fails, try Yellow Pages. Once you have found your band or disco, check what time the musicians or DJ will need to set up equipment, and, if the reception is in a hall or marquee, make sure there are sufficient power points in convenient places for the instruments.

Going Away

After the speeches and cake cutting, the bride and groom have some time to mix with their guests and enjoy their company until they are ready to leave for their honeymoon, or, if there is to be an evening reception, there is often a short break while the room is cleared and re-arranged as necessary. The guests can take the opportunity to rest, take a short stroll and change into a different outfit for the evening if they wish.

At the end of the reception, whether afternoon or evening, the bride and groom may retire to change into their going away clothes (arrangements should have been made in advance regarding a room for this), and the friends of the couple can take the opportunity to 'decorate' the going away car with messages, balloons, ribbons, tin cans and old shoes for good luck. (If the couple are leaving in their wedding attire, this will have to be done earlier.) Before she leaves for her honeymoon, the bride throws her bouquet to the guests. Traditionally, whoever catches it will be the next bride, so it is usually left to one of the bridesmaids or unmarried girls to catch it if possible. The bride and groom make their farewells, and eventually leave in a hail of confetti to bring them luck in their new life together.

When the bride and groom have finally left, the guests will start to depart, thanking the hosts as they leave. If the bride and groom are themselves the hosts but still plan to leave before most of the guests, it would be a good idea to delegate 'someone' – perhaps the 'parents of' or the best man – to make sure that all the guests depart by the time the hall or hotel rooms must be cleared. If the reception is held at home, be prepared for a late night since many relatives and friends will be happy to stay and chat into the small hours after an enjoyable and relaxing day, especially if they haven't seen each other for some time!

'Civil Wedding' Reception

This is such a recent innovation that the bride and groom have the opportunity to plan both the wedding ceremony and the reception to suit themselves. The services offered will vary according to the type of venue, and the couple can arrange 'their day' exactly as they want it to be.

Most hotels and night clubs offering registered premises for a civil wedding have a special room where the marriage ceremony is held, which may be separate from the room used for the reception. After the ceremony, the reception and evening 'do' (if appropriate) goes ahead according to the arrangements decided beforehand with the venue manager, as for any other wedding reception. The couple need to discuss all the details with the hotel or 'wedding' manager to make sure the ceremony and reception can be arranged as they have previously decided. Many registered hotels offer a 'package deal' for civil weddings, which may include the hotel completing the arrangements with the Registrar (although the couple will still have to make the initial arrangements and obtain their own Superintendent Registrar's Certificate for the marriage), use of the wedding room, the afternoon reception and evening party, and overnight accommodation before and/or after the wedding for bride and groom, and wedding guests if required. A deposit is usually required on booking, and the final bill settled before or immediately after the reception.

If the wedding is taking place somewhere other than a hotel or club – stately home, civic building or National Monument, for instance – the owner or manager of the property may offer a complete wedding package including catering for the reception, as in a hotel. Alternatively, they may just offer the use of the building or certain rooms for the ceremony and reception, and supply names of recommended caterers who will arrange the reception directly with the bride and/or her mother. It may be that the bride, the bride's mother or the couple themselves may wish to arrange their own catering or even do it themselves. In this case there will be a charge for the hire of the building or wedding room, but the cost of the reception will be paid directly to the caterers or left entirely to the hosts to arrange as they wish, possibly hiring equipment as for a reception in any hall.

Some venues other than hotels may be able to offer overnight accommodation if required (possibly in self catering units), while others will only have facilities for the ceremony and reception. Some stately homes or civic buildings may only be able to hold weddings on certain days of the week. In some cases the wedding may have to finish by early evening when the venue closes, so that a different venue would be needed for an evening reception, while others have facilities for evening receptions as well as overnight accommodation.

It is most usual for a civil wedding to continue in the same venue for the entire celebration – marriage ceremony, afternoon and evening reception (if there is one), although the bride and groom may prefer to hold a small, intimate marriage ceremony followed by a wedding breakfast with family and very close friends, and then invite other friends and relations to join them later for an evening reception.

Wedding Insurance
It may be sensible to consider taking out some insurance for your wedding, especially if it is being planned some time ahead, in order to alleviate any worries over the wedding arrangements. Many insurance companies offer a complete 'wedding package' covering all aspects of your wedding arrangements and expenses, including cancellation of the wedding or reception due to illness, death, unemployment etc.; closure of the reception venue; problems with the wedding transport and costs of alternative arrangements; theft, loss or accidental damage to 'The Dress' and all other bridal finery, the rings and the wedding presents; unsatisfactory wedding photographs; and public liability for any accidents or damage occurring during 'The Day'.

You may already have home or car insurance, and your company may be able to arrange wedding insurance for you, or the names of insurance specialists can be found in adverts in wedding magazines or through Yellow Pages. The cost is not prohibitive when added to the cost of the wedding, although it may be worth while 'shopping around' for the best quote to suit your particular requirements.

11

STAG NIGHT & HEN PARTY

Before leaving this section on celebrating it seems sensible to mention the traditional (and usually obligatory) Stag Night and Hen Party. Even though they have nothing to do with the reception itself they are very much celebratory events.

The Stag Night is supposed to be the bridegroom's last fling before he says goodbye to the freedom of his life as a bachelor and becomes a respectable married man. It is organised by the groom and best man, and is attended by as many of the groom's male friends and younger male relatives as possible. Traditionally only unmarried men were included but today invitations are extended to the groom's young married friends. Brothers and cousins of bride and groom are also invited, as long as they are old enough to partake of the large quantity of alcohol drunk on such occasions, and the fathers and uncles may also be included, according to the kind of entertainment planned.

The stag night used to be held the night before the wedding, but today most grooms realise this is not a good idea, as they want to enjoy the wedding and not attend it with a hangover, so the stag night is held earlier in the week or on a convenient weekend prior to the wedding day. The format for the stag night is traditionally a gathering in a pub or club, or visits to several hostelries in the area, often followed by a meal in a local restaurant, with many toasts being made and as much alcohol drunk as possible.

A kitty to pay for the drinks can be organised by the best man, and the meal *may be* paid for by the groom, although usually everyone contributes to the cost. Entertainment in the form of a female entertainer or strippergram may be organised by the groom's friends. The best man has the responsibility of ensuring that the groom gets home safely and that the other guests either walk or go home by taxi after the evening's drinking.

Nowadays the stag night has become more sophisticated. It may even extend over a weekend with a visit to a sporting event, a visit to Ireland to drink Guinness, or a day at an entertainment park (where everyone dresses up as soldiers and stalks the opposing team with paint guns!), or may include other interests of the bridegroom.

Not to be outdone, the bride and bridesmaids can organise a hen party or 'girls night out' for the female friends of the bride, usually a more up-market affair than the stag night. It may include a visit to the local pub or wine bar, followed by a meal in a restaurant, possibly with male entertainment (some restaurants will arrange this for you), and a visit to a night club or disco, or it can be a quieter evening at the home of the bride or one of her girl friends, with lots of wine and gossip. Like the men, the girls can also organise a weekend away, possibly a visit to a health or beauty club, sporting event or theatre weekend, with a night in a good hotel.

Sometimes a joint weekend event can be organised, with the two groups 'doing their own thing' on Saturday, and all meeting up for a meal on Sunday before returning home.

PART THREE

Announcing, Inviting & Recording

12

PUBLICITY

Engagement and Forthcoming Marriage Announcements
These can be put into the appropriate columns of national and local press. Although far less common then it used to be, many couples, or their parents, like to do this, especially if families and friends are scattered and may not all have been told the news personally (although you then often have to ring everyone to tell them it's in the paper!). These notices are charged for, and details of prices will be found in the announcement pages of the paper or by telephoning the classified advertisement section of the newspaper office concerned. After the announcement in the paper, be prepared for an avalanche of advertising material from hopeful wedding services, which may, or may not, be helpful and welcomed. National papers which carry Wedding Announcements include *The Times*, *The Daily Telegraph*, *The Guardian*, *The Independent* and *The Scotsman*.

Having decided which newspaper(s) you are going to use, look at the form of announcement and wording used by the paper and write out your own notice. Most announcements include the names of the couple and their parents, and the towns where the parents reside, and may also include the date of the wedding if it is to take place in the near future. Some couples, especially if it is a second wedding, if they intend to host their own wedding, or if they are an older couple, may prefer to make the announcement just in their own names.

Wedding Reports

After the wedding has taken place a report can be put into the announcement columns of local or national newspapers, stating when and where the marriage took place, and giving the names of bride and groom, their parents, best man, bridesmaids and pageboys and any important guests or famous personalities who attended, as well as details of the service, reception and honeymoon destinations. In the local press this may be free but for the national press copy is generally charged by the word or line, so these notices can be quite expensive if you want a full account.

The usual way to place these notices is by phoning the report directly to the paper (the number will be found in the announce-ment section). Have your report written out ready to dictate over the phone, and be prepared to pay by credit card or to send a cheque before the announcement is put in the paper. The copy writer who takes your call will be able to help or advise you on the wording of the notice if you are unsure what to put. Written notices can be sent, with a cheque, direct to the newspaper office. Some papers print an announcement form in their advertising section, which is easy to fill in with the wording required. Deadlines for publication, particularly in the weekly papers, must be observed if you want your notice in for a particular date.

A Wedding Photograph and Short Wedding Report

This is usually free in local papers (counting as copy, not advertising), but your wedding will only appear in the nationals if the bride and/or groom are national celebrities or there is some real public interest in your wedding! The local paper will supply you with a form to fill in brief details of bride, groom, their parents, best man, bridesmaids, pageboys, etc. Wedding photographers usually have these forms ready to give to you when you book their services. Return the completed form to the photographer before the wedding and then he can send it to the paper with his best photograph, or you can send in form and photo yourself if you are not using a professional photographer.

It may be a few weeks before the report appears (often with a number of inaccuracies, as most papers seem unable to copy the details correctly!), according to how much space is allocated to weddings in each edition.

Examples of Forthcoming Marriage Announcements in the National Press

Mr J S Smith and Miss Mary Jane Robinson
The engagement is announced between James Simon, elder son of Mr and Mrs R C Smith of Macclesfield, Cheshire, and Mary Jane, only daughter of Mr and Mrs J D Robinson of Bromley, Kent.

Lieut. Cdr. J S Smith and Miss M J Robinson
The engagement is announced between Lieutenant Commander J S Smith RN, elder son of Captain and Mrs R C Smith of Macclesfield, Cheshire, and Mary Jane, only daughter of Mr and Mrs J D Robinson of Bromley, Kent.

Mr J S Smith and Mrs M J Robinson
The engagement is announced and the marriage will take place quietly in Bromley on July 30th, between Mr James Simon Smith of Macclesfield, Cheshire, and Mrs Mary Jane Robinson of Bromley, Kent.

If either parent is dead
Mr J S Smith and Miss M J Robinson
The engagement is announced between James Simon, elder son of the late Mr R C Smith and Mrs Smith of Macclesfield, Cheshire, and Mary Jane, only daughter of Mr J D Robinson and the late Mrs Robinson, of Bromley, Kent.

If either parents are divorced
Mr J S Smith and Miss M J Robinson
The engagement is announced between James Simon, elder son of Mr R C Smith of Macclesfield, Cheshire, and Mrs S E Smith of Plymouth, and Mary Jane, only daughter of Mr J D Robinson of Bromley, Kent, and Mrs M Brown of Cheltenham.

Examples of Births, Marriages and Deaths columns in Local Papers
These notices are usually less formal than those in the national press, and may be inserted by either family in their local paper.

SMITH-ROBINSON Mr and Mrs Roland Smith of Macclesfield are pleased to announce the engagement of their elder son James Simon to Mary Jane, only daughter of Mr and Mrs J D Robinson of Bromley, Kent.

Or

ROBINSON – SMITH Mr and Mrs J D Robinson of Bromley are delighted to announce the engagement of their only daughter Mary Jane to James Simon, elder son of Mr and Mrs R C Smith of Macclesfield, Cheshire.

Alternative wording for the announcement if either father is dead
......the late Mr R D Smith and Mrs Smith....

If either mother is dead
....Mr R D Smith and the late Mrs Smith....

If the parents are divorced
....son of Mr R D Smith of Macclesfield and Mrs S E Smith of Plymouth, Devon

Or if the mother has remarried
....son of Mr R D Smith of Macclesfield and Mrs S E Green of Plymouth, Devon

Examples of Announcements which may be made in national and local press immediately after the wedding

The marriage took place on 11 September at St Mary's Church, Bromley, Kent, between Mr James Simon Smith, elder son of Mr and Mrs R C Smith of Macclesfield, and Miss Mary Jane Robinson, only daughter of Mr and Mrs J D Robinson of Bromley.

Or

The marriage arranged between Mr James Smith and Mrs Mary Jane White took place quietly in Bromley, Kent, on September 11th.

13

GUEST LISTS &
WEDDING STATIONERY

Invitations, service sheets, place cards, seating plans, menus, wedding present lists, thank-you cards, printed napkins, coasters, books of matches, cake boxes... If you are determined to 'do the thing properly' the list of wedding stationery is seemingly endless. However, it is usual to settle for just a few items, generally invitations, service sheets and place cards.

The Guest List
Before you can buy or order the invitations you need to draw up the guest list. Whom to invite can be a real problem, even causing great friction between families. Do you invite all the relatives on both sides, including those who are only names on Christmas cards, and what about parents' friends who only know bride and groom 'secondhand', work colleagues and small children (this can cause a lot of bad feeling when people expect their children to be included)? What happens if the groom comes from a large family of brothers, sisters, aunts, uncles and cousins who all expect to be invited and the bride is an only child with few relatives? And it gets even more traumatic if either of the couple or their parents have been divorced. The biggest question of all, of course, will be who is going to foot the bill?

Some couples divide the list into two equal parts – bride's side and groom's. Others divide it into three – bride's family, groom's family and the couple's friends. Some couples decide 'absolutely no small children', while other brides want 'yards of pretty little bridesmaids', and invite whole families, including tiny tots. (Be aware that too many children in church and reception can be distracting or even disastrous!) Cutting the names down to a suitable number will need a lot of tact all round and the ideal solution is for the bride and groom and both sets of parents to sit down together over a cup of coffee or bottle(s) of wine to sort out the names and final numbers. In many cases such a meeting will not be possible, and the bride, or the bride's mother, may have to liaise between the groups carefully until a satisfactory conclusion is agreed. You may even need to draw up a reserve list of people to invite if there are any spaces when the first replies come in.

You will also have to decide if there is to be an evening reception too, and, if so, whether all the wedding guests are to be invited to stay on, or, as is becoming more usual, whether you will invite family, close friends and possibly older friends of the parents to the wedding and afternoon reception, and then have a separate evening party and/or disco mainly for the couple's own friends and colleagues. In this case, you will often find that the older people who have been at the wedding, although invited to stay on in the evening, will 'leave it to the youngsters' and go home before the disco starts. This party can be held in the same place as the afternoon reception, or it may be necessary to hold it at a different venue, and this must be made clear on the invitations.

When finally deciding on the numbers for both afternoon and evening receptions, the question of who is going to pay must be raised. Traditionally the bride's parents pay for everything, but nowadays many families share the expense, with the groom's parents and often the couple themselves making a contribution. Wedding receptions are very expensive occasions, and the number of guests and the type of reception must depend on what the families feel they are able to afford.

Invitations

These are usually sent out by the bride's parents who are traditionally the hosts at the wedding, even though the groom's parents often contribute to the costs and organisation. Nowadays many couples, particularly if they're already living together or it's a second marriage, send out the invitations in their own names.

The price of wedding stationery varies tremendously, according to quality and size of the cards. The most expensive cards are personally embossed or printed with full details of the forthcoming wedding, just leaving the name of the guests to be filled in as appropriate, or you can buy cards that request 'your' company, so that there is no need to write anything at all on the card, but this may be regarded as bad form by the traditionalists.

Cards can be ordered from High Street stationers or specialist wedding shops, or look for printers or wedding services in Yellow Pages. They will have albums showing the wide range of styles available, plain or decorated to suit all tastes, and you should compare prices before making your choice. Order printing as early as possible, as printers may need several weeks to complete the order, especially at busy 'wedding times'. There is a lot of snobbery connected with wedding stationery, so make sure everyone approves the final choice. A cheaper alternative is to buy ready made invitations which come in all shapes, sizes and prices, plain or pretty, formal or funny, from any stationer. Filling in all the details in your best handwriting, as well as addressing all the envelopes, can be a mammoth task, especially if you are having a large wedding. Do check that the invitations have RSVP at the bottom, and some invitations include a reply slip, which encourages an early reply.

Artistic couples may prefer to make their own wedding stationery – our groom decided he didn't like the cards available, and so made simple but effective cards using two shades of corrugated card, some string and a heart shaped template. Another couple, already living together, made amusing circular cards, announcing that 'they had at last got around to it'.

You should make it quite clear on the invitations whether guests are invited to the wedding service and afternoon reception only, or to stay on to an evening 'do' as well, or whether the invitation is to an evening party *only*. You will need a different set of invitations if you are holding a separate evening reception with a second set of guests.

It is customary to send invitations to the groom's parents (if the bride's parents are sending out the invitations – or both sets of parents if the couple are hosting their own wedding) – even if all the parents have been involved in the planning and arrangements. All members of both families should also be sent invitations, even if they have already been invited verbally and will be taking part as best man, bridesmaids or ushers. Couples, or families where the children are invited (do for goodness sake make it clear on the invitation if the children are included), can be sent one invitation between them, but older or adult 'children' should receive a separate invitation, including their girl/boy friend or partner, if appropriate. You may like to invite single or divorced friends to bring a partner to the wedding, and their invitation should be filled in '....and partner' or '....and friend'. When they reply, make a note of their friend's name (or find out if it's not mentioned) for use on the seating plan and place card at the reception.

Order or buy more cards than you expect to need, to allow for a few mistakes when writing the invitations, and also for any last minute guests you may wish to invite. The bride and the mothers will also want cards to keep in the wedding albums.

Invitations should be sent out quite early, to give guests plenty of warning to keep that date free (2-3 months ahead is usual), and to allow time for the replies to arrive back in order to finalise the catering arrangements. If you have guests coming from a distance away who will not know the area, it may be useful to draw a small, simple map showing the location of the church or Register Office, reception venue, parking and other relevant information, which can be photocopied and sent out with the invitations. You could also include details of local hotels or B&Bs, and any special deals available at the reception hotel, for guests who will need to stay overnight, or a note (for the privileged) of where they will be 'allocated' rooms with family, neighbours or friends.

Replies to invitations will come handwritten, on the reply slips or on pre-printed cards which the senders will fill in. (If they forget to add their name(s) it can be an interesting process of elimination to work out who sent it!) It is best to keep a clear record of who has replied so that you can see at a glance if you need to check on anyone before you give final numbers to your caterers or hotel venue.

Sample Wedding Invitation Wordings

Mr and Mrs John D Robinson
request the pleasure of the company of
....
at the marriage of their daughter
Mary Jane
with Mr James Simon Smith
at St Mary's Church, Anytown,
on Saturday, 11 September (year) at 12.30pm
and at a reception afterwards at the
Moorland's Hotel

6 Lupin Lane
Anytown
Anyshire   *RSVP*

Alternative wording

If either of the bride's parents are dead
Simply use the full name of the surviving parent:

Mr John D Robinson (or Mrs Margaret Robinson)
requests the pleasure

or start with the space for the name of the guest(s) and then say:

The pleasure of your company is requested
at the marriage of
Mary Jane
daughter of xx and the late xx

If the parents are divorced:

Mr John D Robinson and Mrs Margaret Brown

If the bride and groom are sending the invitations themselves:

Mr James Smith and Miss Mary Robinson
request the pleasure of the company of

....

at their marriage
at St Mary's Church, Anytown

Or, for a more personal wedding:

James and Mary
request the pleasure

Service Sheets

These can also be ordered from most High Street stationers, wedding shops or printers and will have either the whole order of service or just the words of the hymns. If you are having printed invitations, the service sheets can be ordered to match, but once again the shop will have an album of styles from which you can make your choice. Allow one service sheet for each guest, one for each of the wedding retinue – vicar, bride and groom, bride's father, best man, bridesmaids and pageboys – and some spares for the choir and for friends and neighbours who may come to the church although not attending the reception.

Do confirm the service details, music and choice of hymns with the clergyman (and organist) concerned before ordering the service sheets. Obviously the service sheets will have to be personally printed, so great care must be taken to provide the printer with an accurate, spelling-mistake-free copy, for they will expect to print whatever you have written. If you have access to a word processor you can save money by printing your own service sheets, and use best quality paper for very professional results. Ask the clergyman about copyright.

Of course, there is no *need* to go to the trouble and expense of service sheets, although most couples like to add this special touch to their wedding service. Guests can use the hymn and service books available at the church instead, provided the vicar knows in advance that you will need them and can arrange for them to be left out ready for use.

Place Cards

Place cards can be printed to match the invitations or bought in

packets off the shelf or hand made at home, but they will have to
be typed or filled in by hand when all the replies are received.
You will need to find 'someone' who has beautiful, clear
handwriting or uses a calligraphy pen or is a whizz with a
typewriter. Some hotels or restaurants will fill in your cards or
supply place cards for you, if you arrange this and give them the
guest list well in advance. Place cards are not necessary at
finger buffet 'stand up' receptions, but it is much easier at a fork
buffet or sit down meal if everyone is allocated a place to sit, so
that no-one is left sitting alone or wandering round hoping to
find a group to sit with.

Menu Cards
These can be printed professionally or on a word processor, or
bought with the place cards and hand written or typed, as above,
by you or the hotel once the menu has been finalised. One or
two cards per table should be enough (although you may need
more if you have extremely long tables). Alternatively you may
find that the hotel will provide these as part of their service.

Seating Plan
Once the seating plan has been finally agreed by bride, groom
and their parents in what is hoped will be a friendly, peaceable
arrangement, the plan can be printed, typed or hand written,
usually onto a large sheet of paper which is displayed near the
entrance to the hall or dining room, for guests to check as they
come in. You will also need a smaller copy to give to the head
waiter, who may prefer to seat the guests himself, and a copy for
the waiter or 'someone' who is in charge of putting out the place
cards on the tables before the guests go in.

Extras
Paper napkins, books of matches, coasters, wedding cake boxes,
etc., printed with the names of bride and groom and the wedding
date, will need to be ordered well in advance, especially for a
summer wedding when printers are very busy. Caterers usually
provide plain napkins, and plain cake boxes are available at
most stationers, so it is your choice which, if any, of such items
you wish to order.

Wedding Present Lists
Some brides are embarrassed by making a gift list, feeling it is

impolite to suggest that they expect a present. Of course, you
don't send out the wedding list with the invitations, but while
some guests may decide to give the couple a (very welcome)
cheque or a personal gift of their own choice, most people will
ask to see the wedding list in order to buy something the couple
really want and to avoid duplication – the days of receiving ten
toasters are long gone. Also, with so many couples setting up
home together before they get married, it is a help for guests to
know what they really still need. The bride and groom should go
through the house and draw up a list of what they would like to
receive. The gifts can range from the expensive (or hopeful)
house, car, TV set, dishwasher, etc. (you never know, several
members of the family might club together to buy an expensive
item between them), through to the more usual wedding
presents – bed linen, towels, glasses, china, saucepans and
kitchen equipment – and should include some inexpensive items
such as cake tins, cork screw, tin opener, etc., for children, or
acquaintances who 'would like to buy you a little something'.
Put the make, product name or number, colour, style and, where
possible, the name of the shop from where the item is available.

Everyone's list will vary, and if the couple already have a
home together they may like to receive more unusual or luxury
items – a particular picture or ornament, car phone, plants and
garden furniture, camcorder, answerphone, bottles of wine, etc.
– as well as additional or replacement items for their home. The
list can be made out room by room or by each store (we found
this a good way, as people would say 'I'll get something from
Habitat/Debenham's/Lewis's, it's easy for me to go there' and
they would select something from that section).

The bride (or maybe the groom) but often the bride's mother
can then 'manage the list', which means dividing the main list
into several smaller sections with a varied selection of gifts of
all kinds and prices, in order to get 'the list' to all the guests
who ask for it before the wedding. Keep a master copy of the
main list, and cross off items as they are promised, making
another careful list of gifts and their donors as they are received.

The alternative to keeping the list yourselves is to register
with the Wedding List Service now offered, at no charge, by
most large stores. The bride and groom (or bride and her
mother) will need to see the Wedding Consultant in the chosen
store (if your guests are spread throughout the country choose a

store with branches in most towns), and select gifts from the
different departments. The consultant will then compile the
wedding list, send a copy to the couple and keep a master copy
at the store. When a guest wants to choose a wedding gift, they
go to the Wedding Consultant at the nearest branch who will get
the ·updated list up on the computer or faxed through
immediately, so that the guest can make his/her choice in the
store and that item will be crossed off the list. Guests can also
select their gifts directly over the phone from the wedding
consultant at the main store where the list is held, and have it
wrapped and delivered direct to the bride's address if that is
easier.

The wedding present list is the one thing in the wedding
preparations that should not be completed too far ahead, as
stores tend to change the colours and styles of their stock very
frequently, so that, for example, goods chosen in January may
not be available in July when guests may want to buy gifts.
Make up the list just before you send out the invitations, and
check how long colours and styles will be available before
putting them on the list. (Don't be caught out like our bride,
who planned a navy bathroom in May and then discovered that
navy was the winter range and only pale blue was available
when puzzled guests were shopping in July for her August
wedding.)

Suggested Items to Include on a Wedding Present List

Sitting Room	**Bedroom**	**Bathroom**
Clock	Pillows	Towels
Cushions	Duvet	Bath mat
Coffee table	Sheets	Mirror
Lamps	Duvet covers	Linen basket
Video player	Blankets	Bath rack
Television set	Pillow cases	Indoor clothes line
Vases	Bedspread	Bathroom scales
Chairs	Beside clock/tea	Towel rail
Rugs	maker	Soap holder
Settee	Electric blanket	Make-up mirror
CD player	Quilt/throw	Loo brush & holder
	Mirror	Pretty jars for soaps,
	Jewellery boxes	cotton wool, etc.
	Trouser press	

Kitchen

Refrigerator/freezer
Washing machine
Dish washer
Cooker
Food mixer
Electric kettle
Coffee percolator/
   cafetière
Kitchen knives
Bread board
Bread bin
Toaster
Slow cooker
Microwave oven
Sandwich maker
Mixing bowls
Saucepans
Tea towels
Can opener
Kitchen tools
Kitchen scales
Pressure cooker
Storage jars
Trays
Wooden spoons
Washing up bowl
Casserole set
Frying pan
Oven gloves
Spice Rack
Cork screw
Bottle opener
Tumble dryer
Food processor
Measuring jugs
Kitchen stools

Dining Room

Dining table
Dining chairs
Place mats
Tablecloths
Heated trolley/hot
   plate
Dinner service
Tea service
Breakfast set
Salt & pepper mills
Cutlery
Water jug &
   tumblers
Wine glasses
Sherry glasses
Decanters
Sideboard
Cheese board &
   knife
Candlesticks
Coffee set
Coffee mugs
Place mats
Table mats

Miscellaneous

Vacuum cleaner
Carpet sweeper
Brushes & mops
Dustpan & brush
Garden furniture
Garden tools
Wastepaper
   baskets
Mower
Luggage
Car rug
Picnic set
Ornaments
Wine rack
Shrubs & trees
Garden shed
Door mat(s)
Wheelbarrow
Barbecue
Barbecue tools
Shoe scraper
   (hedgehog)
Electric drill
Household tools
Smoke alarm(s)
Answerphone
Car/mobile phone
Sewing machine
Document box/case
Shopping basket/bag
Thermal bag
Thermal flask
Camcorder

Thank-you Cards

Of course, all those lovely gifts should be acknowledged in writing fairly promptly, although a phone call or verbal thank-you is nice as well. If you have a very large number of guests, thank-you cards can be ordered and printed with the invitations, or bought 'off the shelf' from the stationers, and sent out with a personal note from the bride and groom. The thank-you letters should also give the couple's married address, useful if they are moving house on their marriage. Some couples send out newsy computer printed letters when they return from their honeymoon, rather like the family news letters some people enclose with their Christmas cards, but nothing is as nice to receive as a personal, hand written thank-you letter, however brief. Our bride and groom made thank-you cards with a wedding photo on the front, and a short personal letter inside, thus providing a pretty memento for those who were there, and a glimpse of the wedding for those who were unable to attend.

14

WEDDING PHOTOGRAPHS & VIDEOS

The Photographs

These will be expensive; 'think of a number and double it' money!!! Professional wedding photography is now big business, and although photographers offer widely varying coverage of 'The Day', in the end the longer the photographer attends and the more photographs he takes, the price will rise accordingly.

The photographs are a very important part of the wedding day, so you must be really happy and confident with the photographer and like his work or you may be disappointed with the finished results. Contact several photographers to compare their prices, and get a good idea of their work and the services offered. You can find names of local photographers from Yellow Pages (these days not all photographers have studios in the High Street), and study the wedding reports in your local newspaper, as many photographers have their names printed under their wedding photographs. Enquire among your friends and colleagues who have been involved in recent weddings about their experiences, and ask if you may see their finished albums. Get to know as much as possible about the photographer before making your final choice.

Professional photographic coverage can vary, from a minimum of 20-30 photographs in a series (from the arrival of the groom and best man at the wedding venue, traditional poses of the wedding retinue and family groups before and after the ceremony and posing with the wedding cake before the reception), through to a 'full day package' coverage, with detailed timetable and exact list of photos to be taken. For a full day the photographer will arrive several hours before the ceremony, take pictures inside the empty church (if appropriate), visit the homes of bride and groom and record the wedding preparations there, take pictures at the church before, during and after the service, take specially posed photos of bride and groom in a pretty or romantic setting (under a tree in the hotel garden, by a fountain or stream), cover the reception, the speeches, cutting the cake, the evening 'do' if there is one, and finally pictures of the couple leaving on their honeymoon (phew!). This amount of coverage will cost a small fortune, and most people opt for something in the middle of these two extremes. The photographer may bring an assistant (usually female) to attend to details such as showing the wedding dress to its best advantage and arranging the groups artistically where everyone can be seen.

Some photographers take very formal, posed photographs, others prefer to take completely natural, informal shots of the wedding party and wedding guests, while others may take some of each. Our bride and groom wanted a completely informal coverage, and we have a wonderful kaleidoscope of the wedding day, but I would have liked a few formal poses and traditional groups. It is becoming fashionable today to have some, or even all, black and white photographs and some hazy or indoor natural light photographs besides the usual coloured ones, as a change from the bright colours we've all got used to – these will please the 'arty' types but some elderly relatives may mutter 'can't they afford colour?', so discuss this when choosing the photographer, as it would be a shame not to have some record of the carefully chosen colours in the wedding entourage.

The photographs may be presented as contact prints (very small – you need a good magnifying glass!) or proofs, or in a preview album for you to choose from, with finished photos costing extra, or they may be chosen completely by the photographer and presented in the finished album as a full record of the day. Make sure you know exactly what you will be getting for your money, and check deposits required and final payments – some photographers offer a price reduction if paid in advance, but remember you will then have paid in full before seeing any of the photographs.

Having decided what you want – it is *your* day not the photographer's – make sure your chosen photographer knows the exact coverage you expect, and give him a list in advance if you want any particular poses or groups. A good photographer will do everything possible to make the day special for you, so it is important to agree an approximate timetable with him, and be aware that sometimes the photographer gets so involved in his work that he seems to take over the proceedings, painstakingly composing pose after pose outside the church and then whisking the couple away for the 'artistic shots', leaving the disgruntled wedding guests to hang around, sometimes for an hour or more, before the bride and groom reappear and the reception can start.

Lots of the guests will take lovely photos of the wedding which they will send to the couple (although younger members of the family may appreciate an offer to pay for developing!). A friend who is a good and reliable photographer may even be asked to take the formal wedding pictures, but this is a big responsibility and rather restricts the photographer's participation in the partying, so most people prefer to have some professional photographs 'to be on the safe side', as this is a scene that is hard to repeat if by some horrible mishap the film doesn't come out! Costs can always be cut by asking a friend to *supplement* the professional by taking the informal shots of the wedding guests and the reception.

Most churches allow photographs during the signing of the register, but if you want photographs taken during the service this should be agreed beforehand with the vicar, minister or priest. Many churches do not encourage photography, finding the flash a distraction during the service, but may allow natural light photographs if you particularly want them.

Photography in a Register Office must be arranged beforehand with the Registrar, as it is more usual to have photographs taken outside after the wedding rather than during the ceremony – for one thing the number of people in the Register Office is limited due to lack of space. Some Register Offices are situated in very pleasant surroundings, but others are in busy streets and shopping centres, so it may be preferable to have wedding photos taken at the reception venue if it is more suitable.

One tip from hard experience – when getting your own or your family's wedding photos developed, order 'double' or even 'treble' prints. It's so much cheaper at the time than ordering lots of reprints later.

Traditional Wedding Poses and Groups

Before the Service
The church – showing any special features
Inside the church – flower arrangements, stained glass
Groom and Best Man
Groom, Best Man and Ushers
Guests arriving at the church
Bridesmaids and Pageboys waiting for the bride
Bride arriving with her father
Bride, Bride's Father and Bridesmaids

During the Service (on approval of clergymen)
Bride and her father walking down the aisle
Bridal party in front of priest
Taking the vows
Exchanging rings
Blessing at the altar
Signing the register
Bridal party walking back down the aisle

After the Service
Couple in church doorway
Couple outside church
Bride outside church
Couple, Bridesmaids, Pageboys and Best Man
Couple with Bride's parents
Couple with Groom's parents
Couple with both sets of parents
Couple with Bride's family
Couple with Groom's family
Complete wedding group – all the families and guests
Guests throwing confetti
Couple leaving for the reception

At the Reception
The Receiving Line
Bride's Father's speech
Groom's speech

Best Man's speech
Couple cutting the cake
Bride throwing bouquet
Couple leaving the reception

Wedding Video
Most churches will agree to having a video taken during the
ceremony, provided it is done inconspicuously, but they may
make a charge for this. You can have a professional video taken
or ask a friend to take one for you. Your photographer may be
able to arrange for a video to be taken, or you can find someone
through Yellow Pages or by recommendation from your friends.
As with stills photography, agree beforehand what you want to
be on the video and whether you want a video of the reception
as well. Check with the Registrar in advance if you want a video
taken during the ceremony in the Register Office.

In all cases, check and agree prices beforehand, of both the
original recording and copies of the video. If you want to make
your own copies make sure that the professional video camera
operator will sell you the original video or a copiable recording.

PART FOUR
Flowers

15

BOUQUETS, HEAD-DRESSES & BUTTONHOLES

The wedding flowers can be almost cost free, or another very expensive item. The cost will depend on the type and amount of flowers used, which can vary tremendously according to the season, the taste of the bride and the amount you are willing or able to spend on 'window dressing'.

Most brides carry flowers of some kind, whether just a single beautiful bloom from the garden, a posy of wild flowers, a 'proper' florist's bouquet, a decorated prayer book or silk or dried flowers. Flowers for the bridesmaids usually reflect what is carried by the bride, and some brides choose floral head-dresses for themselves and/or the bridesmaids too. It is customary, but not compulsory, for buttonholes to be sported by the groom and chief male guests (best man, ushers, both fathers and close relatives), and often corsages are worn by the mothers.

Flower arrangements in the church can be as simple or elaborate as you wish, and some floral arrangement in the Register Office is usually provided by the Registrar. Flowers for the reception, both floral arrangements and table decorations, need to be discussed and agreed, and even if the reception is not to be held at home, it is usual to have some floral decorations there to make it as attractive as possible for the bridal party and visiting guests.

Bouquets

The Bride

Every bride will have her own dreams and ideas for her bouquet – shape, size, type and colour of flowers, chosen carefully to enhance her wedding dress, and to match or tone with the bridesmaids' dresses. Fresh flowers are traditional at weddings, but nowadays many brides are opting for a complete theme using dried and/or silk flowers, both as bouquets and for decoration at the reception, as these can be made or ordered and put in place in advance, and will last over the hottest summer day without worry of wilting. The bouquet can then be kept as a beautiful memento of the wedding day.

Visit several florists and ask among your friends for recommendations before deciding where to order the bouquets, as prices vary tremendously from shop to shop and the most expensive may not necessarily be the best. Some florists have a book of pictures of their 'set' bouquets in various styles, shapes and sizes at set prices, so that you can order a certain bouquet and know exactly what flowers it will contain and what it will cost. Other florists have an album with photographs of their previous bouquets, and will be happy to discuss your personal likes and dislikes, make suggestions as to what looks good in a finished bouquet, and will create a bouquet to suit you personally – but make sure you agree the approximate cost in advance! Bridal bouquets are now often set on a tiny oasis holder to keep the flowers fresh all day. Our bride was down in the florist's book as 'no carnations, hates gypsophila', and she carried a beautiful bouquet of white roses, pink tinged rosebuds and trailing green flowering ivies.

If you opt for dried or silk flowers, get several quotes for these too. Many florists are expert in arranging these as well as fresh flowers, and some shops deal only with dried or artificial flowers. These can be arranged in a traditional bouquet, or gathered into an informal bunch, again the colours chosen to complement the bridal retinue.

Some brides prefer a very simple arrangement, or perhaps just a beautiful long stemmed rose or two or three traditional wedding lilies. These, too, should be ordered in advance as you will want absolutely perfect blooms. If you decide to choose flowers from your garden, or specially cultivated wild flowers, plan this carefully and have a 'trial run' beforehand, so that panic decisions are not made with bride standing on the lawn in her wedding dress. Make sure that there is 'someone' – bride's mother, aunt, sister or bridesmaid – who will have time to help the bride to see to these flowers on the wedding morning. A prayer book can be decorated with fresh, dried or silk flowers, either by a florist or at home. If you decide to do it yourself, again, have a practice earlier to save a panic at the last moment.

Bridesmaids
Bouquets for the bridesmaids should complement that of the bride and tone to or match the colour of the dresses. Adult bridesmaids often have a smaller version of the bride's bouquet, while little bridesmaids can carry small posies or sprays, decorated hoops or baskets, or decorated muffs at a winter wedding, and the flowergirls can carry small baskets filled with flower heads or petals to strew before the bridal pair. It's wiser not to suggest that pageboys have anything to do with flowers; wearing a 'silly costume' is bad enough! Order bride's and bridesmaids' bouquets together to make sure everything will match on the day.

Head-dresses
Floral head-dresses, with or without a veil, may be chosen just for the bride or for the bridesmaids as well. These must be carefully chosen as they must last all day and not wilt if fresh flowers are used (the florist will advise on your choice), and stay in place without slipping. They must also be comfortable to wear. This is especially important if there are children wearing flower wreaths: try explaining to a 3 year old who says 'the flowers are scratchy' that she's got to keep them on in church. A good florist will advise you which flowers are suitable to use; obviously you will want to complement the wedding dress and bouquet, but some fresh flowers will last better and remain in place more easily than others. Try out your ideas beforehand to avoid any last minute adjustments on the day. Our bride wore tiny white rosebuds and trailing ivy leaves on a comb, and they still looked lovely when she eventually left with her husband just before midnight.

Buttonholes and Corsages
These can be picked from the garden if you have plenty of

flowers at home but it's more usual to order them with the bouquets. A florist will wire the flowers with some greenery if you wish, and wrap the stems so that the flowers stay fresh and can easily be pinned in place. Carnations are the most popular buttonhole flower as they last very well, but you can choose any flower from the bride's bouquet, or to match the groom's tie or waist coat. Our groom chose a rose to match the bride, and that lasted well despite the warm sunshine. I have seen a wedding guest sporting a dandelion, but I think that was just an 'impulse buy'!

If you order flowers for the mothers, it would be wise to check the colours they prefer beforehand, so that there are no embarrassing colour clashes with their outfits.

The Wedding Cake

The traditional topping for the cake is a silver vase holding a few fresh flowers to match the bride's bouquet, or alternatively a small spray of wedding flowers can be laid on the top. If you want this form of decoration, order them to be delivered with the wedding bouquets, and make arrangements for them to be collected by the caterer or cake decorator or ask 'someone' to make sure they are put on top of the cake before the start of the reception.

16

FLOWERS FOR CEREMONY & RECEPTION

Church Flowers

First of all, ask the vicar about the usual arrangements for decorating the church, and as long as the wedding will not take place during Lent, when flowers may not be allowed, the choice of decoration is generally yours. You may be satisfied with whatever flowers happen to be in the church or on the altar that day (a good time to choose, then, is Christmas or Harvest Festival!), or you can choose to deck the church specially for your wedding. Problems may arise if there are several weddings on the same day, when a compromise will have to be reached if you all want different colour schemes, but this can usually be sorted out to everyone's satisfaction, and of course it will be cheaper if several families share the cost of the flowers.

Often there is a church Flower Committee or rota of Church Flower Arrangers, and the best thing is to get in touch with them (the vicar will give you names and phone numbers) to sort out the usual arrangements for decorating the church for weddings. You may want to engage a professional florist to take over all the floral decorations (expensive), or the church ladies may do the decorating for you, or you may want to do it yourself.

Church decorating is quite a daunting task unless you are experienced in such matters – what looks good at home may look most insignificant in a church. I was delighted (and relieved) when our church arrangers took over for us, and decked the beautiful old Cotswold stone church with our bride's choice of white flowers – gladioli, lilies, roses, spray carnations, daisies and different flowering ivies – set off with lots of greenery. Ivy was twined round the pew ends and the pulpit, and a floral garland hung over the church door. It looked lovely. We paid for the actual flowers but there was no charge made by the flower arrangers, although a contribution to church funds is always welcomed. Individual churches may have different arrangements.

Discuss exactly what you would like with whoever is arranging the flowers; it's best to do this in the church itself, so that you can picture 'in situ' what you will actually see. Obviously the more arrangements you choose, the more flowers will be needed and costs will rise accordingly.

Suggested Flower Arrangements for the Church
Flowers on the altar
Tall pedestal vases by the altar steps
Vases by the chancel steps where the marriage takes place
Vases at either side at the end of the aisle
Flowers on or around the font
Garlands or flowers on pew ends
Garland or flowers around or on the pulpit
Garland over church doorway
Vases in church porch and in the side chapels

Register Office Flowers
There is usually a floral arrangement on the Registrar's table, but if you have a particular wish for a special arrangement, or for extra flowers in the room, you may be able to provide your own arrangements if you discuss this beforehand with the Registrar, who will try to make your wedding as personal and as special for you as possible.

Civil Weddings
Floral arrangements for a civil wedding will vary according to where it is taking place. The flowers may be provided by the management of the registered premises, and you should discuss with them exactly what is usually provided and what kind of decorations you would like. Alternatively the flowers may be the responsibility of the caterers (see Flowers for the Reception) or you may wish to provide the flowers yourself, as for a church wedding.

Flowers for the Reception

Hotel, Restaurant, Club or Function Room

Enquire what floral arrangements will be provided when booking the venue and decide if you need to ask for extra flowers, and, if so, check what they will cost. Some hotels will decorate the room using your choice of flowers included in the cost of the reception while others will charge extra for a special service.

Table decorations may be included in the price of the catering, but ask what kind of arrangements there will be (two carnations in a wine bottle may be fine for a bistro but you may prefer something a bit more elaborate!). Some hotels will be happy to provide what you want as part of the reception, others will charge extra or suggest that you provide the table decorations yourself.

Hall or Marquee

You can order floral decorations from a florist – preferably the one who is doing the bridal bouquets in order to carry the same colour scheme through – or you can decorate the whole place yourself with help from family and friends. For this you can use flowers bought from the florist or market, or from your own garden.

Arrangements for a hall need to be large and spectacular. All kinds of containers (even buckets, large jugs or dishes) can be used, with a large block of oasis (obtainable from any florist's) to hold the flowers steady, and plenty of greenery to hide the bases. If you prepare the flowers carefully by cutting 1cm ($^1/_2$") off the stems and giving them a long drink in a deep bucket of water before using them, you should be able to do all the arrangements the day before. The flowers will remain fresh provided they are stored in a cool place overnight, although roses (so popular) can be difficult to keep and are best added to an arrangement at the last minute.

Marquee decoration needs to be especially eye catching. You may be brave enough to do it yourself or you may feel happier paying a professional to do it for you. The arrangements are usually hung onto the marquee poles or can be suspended like chandeliers from the 'ceiling'. In such a large area the decorations need to be huge and somewhat overstated for the best effect; one large arrangement is better than two or three small ones. We had a huge arrangement of white flowers and greenery, as in the church, suspended from the central pole of our marquee and twining almost down to the ground, which looked quite spectacular. The marquee company will put up hooks or nails in suitable places for the decorations but are unlikely to provide the floral decor themselves, although they may be able to give you the name of a suitable florist who often does flowers in 'their' marquees.

At Home

Don't forget the floral arrangements in your own home, not only if you are holding the reception there but as a background for the bridal party leaving the house. Many photographers also like to visit both the bride and groom at home to take photos of preparations on the wedding morning before the service. You will have lots of visitors before and after the wedding, with people bringing presents and calling to wish bride and groom good luck, so you may like to have the floral arrangements in place a day or two before the wedding. You can do your own flowers or order some arrangements from the florist – lovely arrangements of fresh or dried flowers in baskets or containers ready to stand on table or shelf are now available. Discuss what you want when you order them, it certainly saves you a lot of time at the last minute. Of course, dried flowers can be arranged weeks in advance, either at home or by a professional, which is a great advantage as they can be put in place early, and will need no attention on the day itself.

Table Decorations

Once again it is nice to carry the wedding flower scheme through onto the tables. If the table flowers are being provided by the hotel or caterer, discuss the arrangements with them well in advance, to make sure you are happy with what is offered. If you decide to do them yourself or with help from friends, decide who will collect the flowers and greenery ordered in advance from the florist, and where and when the arrangements are going to be assembled and stored, or transported to the reception venue. Dried flowers, of course, can be arranged well in advance, but fresh flowers can only be done the day before with carefully prepared flowers (as for the other floral arrangements). Leave the finished arrangements in a cool place overnight, ready to be placed on the tables next day.

Don't make the arrangements too big, as buffet and dining tables are crowded with food, plates and far more glasses than usual. Our bride chose unusual decorations which we did ourselves very easily – small trailing ivy plants in little terracotta pots, with white candles to be lit in the evening, and a few fresh white rosebuds arranged amongst the ivy leaves which looked very pretty. Garlands of fresh greenery draped around the table-cloths really need to be done on the day, as they may wilt in a warm room overnight, although garlands of dried flowers can be prepared well in advance and put in place whenever convenient.

Outside

I was lucky as our bride and groom announced their wedding date just before I planted out the summer bedding in the garden and containers. Knowing we were having the reception in a marquee in my garden I was able to continue the 'white wedding' theme there with white petunias, Busy Lizzies, geraniums and pale pink fuschias, with lots of greenery in the tubs, and pastel asters and snapdragons to give some colour. Nearer the time gaps in flower beds can be filled with bought potted plants from garden centres, either left in the (carefully hidden) pot or planted out. Friends and neighbours will usually rally round too. I was able to borrow several lovely tubs to group around the front door (thank you Nora!), and you could place some at the entrance to the marquee or hall to welcome your guests to the reception. Even a rather austere church entrance can be enhanced with some tubs of flowers by the door to brighten up the photographs as the newly weds come out of church, but check this out with the vicar beforehand, and arrange for one or two strong men with a suitable car or van to bring the tubs and remove them to safety afterwards if the church is in a busy city street.

PART FIVE
Bridal Finery

17

THE BRIDE

No matter who is helping with, or even taking responsibility for, the other wedding arrangements, it is for the bride alone to decide how she wants to look on 'The Day'. Therefore the choice of 'The Dress', accessories and the bridal retinue can only be made by the bride herself, although she will usually value some help and advice when making her final decisions. Indeed, once the engagement is announced, even if the wedding date is set many months ahead, most brides-to-be can't resist browsing through the fashion pages of the wedding magazines, and also enjoy the excuse to window shop in wedding dress departments, often with a group of friends or work colleagues to give encouragement.

The Wedding Dress
Lots of factors will affect your choice of dress: where will the service be held, a grand Cathedral setting, a little country church, a Register Office or a Civil Ceremony in a hotel or other venue? Is it going to be a white wedding? Will it take place in summer or winter? Do you want to wear a long or short dress? Do you dream of floating down the aisle in a froth of tulle and lace, or would you prefer a slinky satin creation with an enormous train or a simple cotton broderie Anglaise dress? This is the time to consider as many ideas as possible; most little girls have 'played at weddings' at some time or other and now it's even better – it's for real!

Go and have a wonderful time trying on some of the styles you like, and even some you've not previously considered (you may be pleasantly surprised) and so get a general feel of some of the styles available. After all, for most girls buying a wedding dress is a once-in-a-lifetime experience, so make the most of it!

One of the most important factors in the choice of 'The Dress' must be 'The Price', or how much you (or your parents) are willing to pay in order to get married in the dress of your dreams. This will obviously be determined by whether the dress is to be an exclusive design with a famous designer label, bought ready to wear in a department store or wedding boutique, made to measure by a wedding dress specialist or made at home. Other options to consider are hiring, buying second hand or borrowing from a friend. Some brides feel that for this one special day they will splash out and buy exactly what they want, while others refuse to spend the earth on a dress which will only be worn for a few hours. Whatever your final decision, it really is true that every happy bride looks wonderful on her wedding day, no matter what she is wearing and how much it cost.

Buying
There are good wedding dress departments in most big clothes stores, and specialist wedding shops and boutiques in most towns and cities. These will stock a large selection of dresses in a wide range of colours (white, cream and ivory being most popular, with the occasional pastel or champagne) and prices. You may find rails of the same or similar dresses, which can be a bit off-putting – but does that matter? You're hardly likely to find anyone else wearing a wedding dress at your wedding!

Some dresses are sold straight off the rail, while other shops keep stock dresses for customers to try on, and then make new dresses, either stock size or to your own measurements, for each bride. If you buy a dress off the rail, make sure it's unmarked, with no trace of lipstick or make-up round the neck. It's also worth looking on the reduced rail which often includes end-of-season dresses in perfect condition, but don't buy a dress because it's a bargain unless it is exactly what you want. Most of these shops will have an alterations service, for which a charge is generally made, and you may need to hire or buy a hooped petticoat according to the design of the dress.

When you set off on a serious buying expedition, try and

allow plenty of time for a leisurely choice. If possible, go during the week when the shops will be less crowded and the assistants will have more time to attend to you. It is often worth ringing to make an appointment so that you do not have to hang around for an available assistant, especially if you're shopping at weekends. Take along a friend of your own generation (possibly a bridesmaid) to give an unbiased opinion, as well as your mother who may insist on going anyway (and will be very hurt if not invited) and will think you look lovely in everything! You may be glad of a committee to give you that extra bit of confidence needed for such an important purchase. Listen to the advice of a helpful shop assistant, who will have a wider experience of wedding dresses than you, but be aware that her taste may be different from yours, and she may be working on commission.

When trying dresses on you will need to consider the underwear and shoes you intend to wear on 'The Day'. Both of these will affect the style of dress you choose, so do not make your final decision until you can try the dress with the style of bra or corselette and height of shoe heel you think you will be wearing. You might be surprised what a difference it makes to the look of the dress! (See also pages 115 and 116.)

Incidentally, wherever you buy your dress, don't fool yourself that a traditional wedding dress can be dyed or altered after the wedding to be worn as a ball gown or 'posh frock'. Whatever you do with it, a wedding dress still looks like a wedding dress, so this is almost certain to be a once-only wear!

Designer Dresses
Couturier boutiques can be found in towns and cities, and tucked away in little villages. These shops will stock more exclusive styles and designer label dresses, and will have a designer who will consult with you and design a dress to suit you personally, or will create a dress from your own sketches or photographs. These services can be quite expensive, and the more costly the fabric and elaborate the design, the higher the price. An appointment may be necessary to meet the designer.

Wedding Fayres and Wedding Dress Sales
These events, which usually take place in a hotel or public hall, are where you may (or may not – depending on what you are looking for!) find a bargain. Be careful not to be carried away

by the general euphoria and enthusiasm of the sales people or you may come away having spent more than you intended on a dress with which you are disappointed when you get it home. (Or you may be in danger of buying a 'real bargain' which isn't what you want at all, just because it's cheap.)

Made To Measure

The dress may be designer commissioned with a specialist couturier, ordered and made at a specialist wedding shop or made to measure from a standard design on sale in the wedding dress department, as detailed above. There are also numerous wedding dressmakers who specialise in making wedding dresses and outfits for the whole entourage, and they are well worth considering if you want to wear something a little bit different without paying the earth, although with all the time and work involved the dress will still not be cheap.

The dressmaker may work from a wedding shop or have her workroom in her own house, and can be found from adverts in local papers, wedding magazines, postcard adverts in the paper shop and by personal recommendation. A good dressmaker will have plenty of pattern books and magazines to help you make your choice, and will be able to suggest designs to suit you. She may be able to design a dress for you from your own ideas or work from sketches, pictures or photographs. Some dress-makers keep a stock of fabrics in the workroom, others prefer you to buy your own material and will be able to advise you what to buy and where to find it.

Making at Home

You may be lucky and have a talented mother, sister or friend who is able and willing to make the dress, either from a pattern or your own design, or you may be able to make your own dress if you have enough confidence in your own ability, and 'someone' to help with the fitting. The availability of wedding fabrics varies, and you may have to visit a large store to get a reasonable choice of patterns, materials and decorations. Hooped petticoats, if needed, can be hired from wedding shops.

Hiring

There are specialist Wedding Hire shops in most towns, where you can hire complete outfits for the bride and bridal retinue, as well as morning suits for the men and 'mother of' outfits. Some bridal shops and wedding departments (including the chain stores) also have dresses for hire. Prices vary according to the value of the dress, and whether it is brand new or has been worn before, so that even hiring a dress can be expensive but it certainly won't cost as much as buying the equivalent dress outright. Most shops will do minor alterations to ensure a perfect fit.

Arrangements for hiring vary, but usually the dress can be collected a few days before the wedding and returned soon afterwards. You may have to leave a deposit when ordering the dress and pay the full cost when it is collected. If the dress has been worn before it will obviously have been cleaned and be in brand new condition when you pick it up, and you may have to forfeit the deposit if the dress is marked or damaged when it is returned.

Borrowing
You may have a friend or relative who is happy to lend you her dress, or your mother may have her dress carefully tucked away in the attic and would be delighted to see it put to good use again. Provided not too much alteration is needed, borrowing can be an excellent arrangement. The dress will need cleaning to ensure it looks fresh and clean on the day, and this should only be entrusted to a specialist dry cleaning service – enquire at your local dry cleaners or look in Yellow Pages. If you can't undertake any necessary alterations yourself, a specialist wedding shop or dressmaker may be able to do them for you. Our bride chose to wear a traditional dress, a froth of silk embroidered tulle that had been stored away in tissue paper for over 30 years, and she looked lovely.

Buying Second Hand
There are wonderful bargains to be had through the small ads in the local paper, but it's a case of finding a style you like in your size. Wedding dresses can also be found for sale in charity shops. These dresses may come complete with veil and head-dress, and there may be bridesmaids' outfits on offer too. If the dress has not already been cleaned you may need to arrange specialist cleaning as above.

Head-dress and Veil

These are available to buy or hire at wedding shops, with the dress, or there are specialist head-dress departments in large stores. It is sensible to buy the dress, head-dress and veil together, to ensure a colour match and be sure that the head-dress complements the dress. Numerous styles of head-dresses can be found, from the family tiara (if you're lucky enough to have one), to one of the lovely modern head-dresses, or a specially designed floral head-dress using silk, fresh or dried flowers – these will have to be ordered and made up by the florist (see page 103).

Veils are not compulsory for brides, although they do look lovely and it's probably the only chance you'll have to wear one! The veil is held in place by the head-dress, so make sure the head-dress feels comfortable and holds the veil securely as you're going to be wearing it for quite a long time and need to feel confident and relaxed. Part of the veil can cover your face if you wish (a good idea as it gives you a little privacy at a very emotional time), so make sure the head-dress allows for the veil to be thrown back at the appropriate time.

Certain styles of dress will look best with a beautiful hat instead of a head-dress, and that may be found in the wedding shop or in a specialist hat shop, where you may also find a milliner who will design and make a 'one off' hat especially to go with your dress.

Hair Styles

It's a good idea to try out different hair styles for the wedding with your hairdresser and discuss styles of head-dress that will suit you before buying one. Then have a trial run with bridal hair style and head-dress before the day. The wedding morning is not the time for experiments!

Other Accessories

Underwear

Buy your wedding bra or corselette when you buy your dress and wear it when you have your fitting. Many wedding dresses have a tight bodice and nipped in waist, a style not worn so often in these days of jeans and tee-shirts, so you may have to buy different underwear from that which you normally wear.

Most dresses look best over a strapless bra, and a strapless corselette will nip in your waist amazingly, but don't have it too tight – it's got to feel comfortable all day. The corselette can be worn with suspenders if you're wearing stockings, or you may be more comfortable with bra and suspender belt or choose hold-up stockings for a summer wedding, or tights if it's chilly.

There are beautiful wedding tights and stockings on sale (white or cream, plain, embroidered or lacy) which look lovely with white or cream wedding shoes. Although these may be expensive, it's sensible to buy two pairs in case of an accident on the wedding morning.

Shoes
Wedding shoes must be comfortable since you'll be doing a lot of standing over a long day. As with the underwear, the shoes may be a different style from your usual footwear (no, you can't spray your Doc Martins white to wear under your dress!), so unless you're used to very high heels, it's wise to opt for a medium or low-heeled shoe, no matter how tall the bridegroom! It is important to try the shoes on with the dress for any final fitting to make sure that the hem-line is right for the shoe and, again, you must check the colour in daylight against the dress. Wear the shoes in around the house to get used to them and ensure they'll be comfortable.

Jewellery
The traditional bridal necklace is a string of beautiful pearls, but what you wear will depend on the style of dress and your personal taste. If you're wearing a head-dress and veil, small ear-rings will probably be all that are needed. The bride should keep her left hand free of any jewellery and wear her engagement ring on her right hand for the wedding ceremony, until the wedding ring is safely on her wedding finger. The engagement ring can be changed back to the left hand later in the day.

One last thought on wedding accessories: don't forget the traditional blue trimmed wedding garter to fulfil the rhyme – something old, something new, something borrowed, something blue and a silver sixpence in my shoe.

18

BRIDESMAIDS & PAGEBOYS

Here, again, the bride is likely to have the biggest say in deciding what the look of the outfits for the bridesmaids should be. However, do not get too carried away and remember that bridesmaids (and Matrons of Honour) come in all shapes, sizes, colourings and ages, and, if a large entourage is planned, finding dresses to suit everyone can require a great deal of tact and diplomacy. (It may even require bribery in the case of teenage bridesmaids or some pageboys!)

Unless you have an enormous amount of stamina it's not a good idea to shop for the wedding dress and bridesmaids' outfits, etc., on the same day. You may all get so tired you may not make the right decision and could be disappointed later.

Dresses for Older Bridesmaids

Although most wedding dresses still tend towards the traditional style (long and white!), styles for bridesmaids have become more varied – anything goes, and you can choose from 'normal' dresses that can be worn after the wedding day as well as the long, full-skirted pastel coloured 'bridesmaid's dress' which looks lovely on the day but isn't much use afterwards.

Traditionally the bride and her mother bought the dresses, but it is becoming most usual for the bridesmaids to pay for their own dresses, or at least make a contribution (bride buys material, bridesmaid pays for the making up), particularly if the bride chooses a style and colour that can be worn successfully in the future, possibly as a 'posh frock' or ball gown.

Once the look for the wedding retinue has been agreed by all concerned, the dresses can be bought, hired or made to measure, as for the wedding dress. Wedding shops will have a range of more traditional bridesmaids' dresses, but if you want a more unusual style it may be easier to choose material and get the dresses made by a dressmaker or made at home. (Making a bridesmaid's dress is not as daunting a task as tackling a wedding dress.)

Many traditional brides choose a simpler version of their own style of dress, but without the hooped skirts (too many hoops will look like a chorus from Gilbert and Sullivan!) but every bride will have her own ideas. However, the varied shapes, colourings and tastes of all the bridesmaids must not be ignored in pursuit of the bride's idea of the dream look for her retinue. Bridesmaids can be quite vocal about what they will (or will not) wear, but in the end it is the bride's day and she should have the casting vote.

Head-dresses

Head-dresses for the bridesmaids can be as varied as those for the bride although usually something fairly simple is chosen to complement the bridesmaids' hairstyles. The head-dresses can be bought or hired with the dresses, or bought separately from a wedding shop if the dresses are being made at home. Floral head-dresses must be ordered from the florist with the bridal flowers.

If possible, the bridesmaids should try out their wedding hairstyles with the head-dresses in consultation with their hair-dressers before the wedding. Our adult bridesmaid looked stunning in a short, straight, ivy green silk dress with shoe string straps (perfect for a hot summer day), with a big ivory coloured cloche hat trimmed with the green silk. She carried a posy of ivory rosebuds and tiny ivy leaves, complementing the bride, and was able to wear her dress again as a dinner dress after the wedding.

Other Accessories

Underwear

As with the bride, adult bridesmaids may need strapless bras or corselettes, depending on the style of dress. Again, it is very important to try the dress with the underwear *before* the day of the wedding to make sure that it is appropriate.

Shoes and Stockings

These must be comfortable for the wearer and a good match to the dress. All the comments about the bride's shoes apply equally to those of the bridesmaids (see page 116).

Wedding stockings or tights are available in many variations and there should be spare pairs for emergencies on the day.

Little Bridesmaids and Flowergirls
Little bridesmaids and flowergirls look lovely in almost anything from angelic white and pale colours to gorgeous bright or deep shades. Whatever you choose, make sure the children feel comfortable – no scratchy petticoats or fabrics that irritate – and make sure that long dresses are well above the ankle to avoid tripping up. Head-dresses must be light and easily secured in place and shoes very comfortable; ballet shoes or light sandals are a good choice. If the outfits are hired, check out these points when trying them on, for if the child is uncomfortable she won't be happy, and that can spoil the service for everyone. Make sure that whatever the children are going to carry (posies, baskets, hoops, muffs, etc.) are light and easy to hold, and that they can manage easily with what may be a different type of dress from their normal wear.

Pageboys
Pageboys are a different kettle of fish from the little bridesmaids. Have you ever met a small boy happy to be dressed like Little Lord Fauntleroy? While reluctantly consenting to wear a kilt, sailor suit or even miniature morning dress, most little boys would be utterly mortified at being forced into taffeta, satin or velvet (what if anyone from school should see them?) and bribery may be needed, if pageboys are of school age, to ensure a trouble-free day!

Pageboy outfits are usually 'one off' wear (unlike little bridesmaids' dresses which will be worn as party frocks as long as possible), and are often hired from wedding shops, or may be made to measure with the bridesmaids' dresses. Make sure the pageboy is comfortable in his clothes, and that the shoes in particular are suitable and comfortable – hired black patent pumps with silver buckles might *look* wonderful but may not suit chubby EE fitting feet used to wearing trainers. Men and boys remove their hats in church, so it's probably better not to bother with hats for pageboys – they'll only lose them. If possible, arrange to have the outfits a few days before the wedding so that the boys can have some practice in wearing what may, for them, be rather unusual outfits.

19

OUTFITS FOR THE MEN

There's not a great deal one can say about men's outfits for a wedding – it's usually either morning dress or lounge suits and that's it! The bridegroom (or the bride!) should decide which is going to be worn and then the groom, best man, 'fathers of' and ushers should wear the same. (It is worth remembering that if the bride is wearing a formal dress with a very long train the groom may look somewhat under-dressed in an ordinary lounge suit.) If it's a 'topper and tails' wedding, some of the male guests may also wear morning dress, but usually most of the men wear lounge suits or a dark blazer or jacket and trousers.

Morning Dress
Traditional wear at a formal white wedding, morning suits are usually hired as they are expensive to buy and many men only wear them occasionally. Traditional black morning dress consists of a black tail coat, black or grey striped trousers, grey waistcoat, white shirt (with optional stiff collar), grey silk tie or cravat and grey top hat and gloves. Grey morning dress (grey tail coat, plain grey trousers and waistcoat) is slightly less formal and a good choice for summer weddings, as worn by our bridegroom. There are a variety of others available – such as charcoal grey and even royal blue – and different hire companies have slightly different styles, so it may be worth looking at the suits held by more than one firm before making your choice.

A silk or brocade waistcoat can be worn instead of the grey (perhaps only by the groom and best man to distinguish them from the ushers?), with a matching or contrasting tie or cravat.

Morning suits are worn with dark socks and black shoes. Make sure the shoes are comfortable and 'worn in' if new, and check that the groom has peeled the price off the underside of new shoes, or else it will show when he is kneeling at the altar.

Make sure the whole entourage knows what colour morning dress is to be worn so that they will all wear the same. Morning suits can be hired from many menswear shops and specialist wedding shops and prices vary, so it's worth shopping around. If possible, hire all the suits from the same place, then you will be sure of getting everything to match, and collection and return will be easier – perhaps the best man or one of the fathers can collect the lot and distribute them to the gentlemen concerned.

If groom, best man, ushers and 'fathers of' are scattered around the country it may be best to hire from a company with branches nationwide. These often offer a service whereby each man can be fitted at his local branch and the details are then sent to one chosen branch from which all the required suits are collected. Again, this ensures that all the suits match because they will all be coming from one place and there will be no danger of someone turning up in the wrong style of suit!

It is sensible to try on and reserve the suits early, two or three months in advance, as shops get very booked up at weekends, especially in spring and summer, and when events such as Royal Ascot are taking place. The groom must decide if the men will have top hats and gloves (not usually worn, only carried – and often mislaid), as these will be hired with the suits. Ties or cravats, white shirts and black shoes can all be hired if necessary. A deposit is required on booking and the hire price paid in full when the suits are collected, generally a couple of days before the wedding. Arrangements must be made to pick up the suits, distribute them to the wearers and to collect and return them afterwards. Most firms require them back promptly as they have to be cleaned ready for the next hire booking.

A Word of Warning!

One suit looks very much like another, so if you have several male members of the family getting ready in the same house, make sure their suits and accessories are kept separate to avoid any panic mix-ups on the day. Take suits out of boxes or bags and hang them up as soon as you get them home, and unwrap and iron new shirts (all those pins and they always look creased when unwrapped!), and put ties, shoes, socks and underwear ready to put on too. Check that everyone who needs them has a pair of cufflinks to hand or put ready in the shirt cuffs.

Uniform

If the bridegroom is in the Services – Army, Navy, Air Force, Royal Marines, Merchant Navy, Police, Fire Brigade or any other uniformed service – he may choose to get married in dress uniform. It is likely that the best man and some of the ushers will also be in uniform, as will other friends and colleagues of the groom who are invited to the wedding. If the bride and groom's fathers are not in the services, they will wear dark morning dress or dark lounge suits, as will any un-uniformed ushers and other male guests.

Lounge Suits

Many men dislike, or refuse to wear, morning suits, preferring to 'get married in their own clothes', and decide to wear a lounge suit for the occasion. The choice of colour is entirely personal, with dark grey, black or dark navy, either plain or with a small stripe, being most usual, although paler colours (beige, fawn or light grey) are equally suitable for a more informal or summer wedding. Dark brown is not often worn, as for some reason it is not looked on as a 'formal occasion' colour. It looks nice if groom, best man, ushers and 'fathers of' all wear either dark or light coloured suits. Suits can be made to measure by a bespoke tailor, bought ready to wear, or hired. Alternatively the groom may already have a suitable suit, in which case make sure it is cleaned and pressed to ensure it looks really good on the day.

Buttonholes

The men in the wedding entourage and any important family members (uncles or grandfathers) usually wear a flower in the buttonhole of their suit jacket, which should be ordered with the wedding flowers, or picked from the garden if you wish. Arrangements must be made for the buttonholes to be distributed on the wedding morning: the bride's father will need his at the house, but the others can be distributed at the church by the best man or chief usher before the service.

20

'MOTHERS OF'

The Outfit

Shopping for 'The Outfit' can be the thing that mothers of the bride and groom dread the most. They want to look very special (the wedding of a son or daughter doesn't happen every day), but finding exactly what's wanted, at the right price, can be very difficult. While not being a part of the actual wedding retinue, the mothers will be very much on show and will, of course, be in the photographs, so they may like to choose outfits that complement the colour scheme and don't clash with the bridesmaids, or each other.

The outfit can be made to measure at a specialist wedding shop, by a dressmaker, or made at home; there are always lots of ideas in wedding magazines and pattern books. Alternatively, a smart outfit could be bought in a favourite shop, preferably one with helpful assistants who will give an honest opinion and not hassle their clientele into styles which don't suit them. If a 'mother of' happens to see the perfect outfit in a shop window she would be wise to go in straightaway and try it – it's no good going back a month later and being disappointed to find that it's already been sold.

Specialist wedding shops may also hire out complete outfits, including the hat. The important thing is for the outfit to be comfortable and the wearer to be happy in it: they should not be bullied into something that doesn't feel right just because it's 'fashionable'.

Hats and Hairstyles

This is the time for the 'mothers of' to indulge in a really gorgeous hat, which can be great fun if it's not their usual wear. They can be expensive items, and some hat shops now run a hire service which means that a more expensive hat can be worn than if it was being bought. Some hat shops will also design and make a hat to order, or trim one of their standard designs to match an outfit, often at a very reasonable price.

The hats having been chosen, they should be taken by each 'mother of' to their hairdresser to decide a suitable hairstyle for the day well in advance. After all, they will still want their hair to look good when they eventually remove the hat!

Shoes and Accessories
Shoes should be smart but comfortable – there's a lot of standing to be done! – and they should be worn in beforehand. Matching or complementary handbag and gloves (if worn) should be bought in plenty of time and it's useful if the 'mothers of' keep tissues, comb, lipstick, spare glasses, purse, etc. ready in the bag. Stockings or tights should also be bought (including a spare pair) and underwear, so that everything is to hand when needed.

Jewellery
What jewellery is to be worn should be decided in advance and kept ready to avoid last minute panics on the day.

Corsage
'Mothers of' may wear a floral corsage pinned to dress, jacket or handbag. These can either be ordered with the wedding flowers, the bride having ascertained what colours will be suitable, or each mother may prefer to organise her own corsage. Be clear as to who is ordering it, though, or you could end up either with two for each mother... or without any at all!

21

OTHER CONSIDERATIONS

Register Office Weddings

Bridal finery at the Register Office can range from the traditional white wedding with topper and tails, or the bride in a formal day dress or suit, to the very casual jeans and sweatshirt outfit. As long as they have the necessary licence and two witnesses, anything goes!

Many brides, especially if it is their first wedding, opt for the glamour of a white wedding dress, complete with veil, head-dress and bouquet. If this is the chosen option, a simple style of dress would be most appropriate, without a hooped skirt or long train which might be difficult to manoeuvre around a crowded office. The bride can be attended by bridesmaids, as at a church wedding, and bridegroom, best man and male guests can wear morning dress or lounge suits (or casual wear), as they wish.

The bride not wearing a traditional wedding dress can still achieve the bridal look by wearing a white, cream or pale coloured dress, with a pretty head-dress or hat (bought or hired), and a small bouquet or corsage of flowers. Suits – the traditional outfit for the Register Office wedding – are still popular today, especially if it's a second wedding, as many girls find a suit more useful to wear afterwards than a formal dress. If the bride is not wearing a traditional wedding dress, the groom would wear a lounge suit or more casual wear, not morning dress.

Service of Blessing

If this follows on directly from the Register Office, the couple will obviously wear what they wore at the marriage ceremony, with guests dressing as for any church wedding. However, if the Service of Blessing is held weeks or days (or even a few hours later on the same day) after the civil ceremony, the bride may choose to wear a completely different outfit – perhaps saving the 'traditional' wedding dress for this service.

The groom should take his lead from the bride as to what he should wear. If she is wearing a traditional wedding dress, he may wear morning dress or a dark lounge suit. However, if the bride wears a day dress, suit or more casual wear, the groom should accompany her wearing a lounge suit, blazer, jacket and trousers, or more casual attire, as appropriate.

Evening Reception

Dress for this may vary according to whether the same guests stay on for the evening after the wedding reception, or whether it is a completely separate 'do', with guests arriving dressed for an evening's dancing or disco entertainment. The bride will usually stay in her wedding dress for at least the beginning of the evening reception so that the guests who did not attend the wedding service will have a chance to see the dress. She can then change later into her going away outfit.

Some brides may prefer to change into something more suitable for dancing or more casual for the evening reception, but most brides are determined to wear their wedding dress for as long as possible – after all, they won't be wearing it again! If the bride is going to wear a different outfit for the evening, arrangements must be made to take it to the reception venue earlier in the day. Don't forget shoes and underwear, as you'll probably need something different from what was worn with the wedding dress.

As with the bride, the bridesmaids often wear their dresses at the evening reception, to give all the guests a chance to admire the bridal retinue. They may choose to change into different outfits later, and in this case you must make arrangements (again, as for the bride), to deliver them to the reception venue earlier.

If the bride is staying in her wedding dress, the groom should stay in his wedding attire until the bride goes to change. Then, like the bride, he can change into his going away outfit or something more casual for the rest of the reception.

The 'mothers of' may stay in their wedding outfits for the evening reception, or may prefer to change into something suitable for dancing or a more casual outfit. Here again, everything should be put ready in advance and taken to the evening venue earlier in the day.

Best man, ushers and 'fathers of' may stay in their wedding attire or change into something more casual or suitable for dancing, usually following the wishes of the bride!

'Going Away' Outfits

Traditionally bride and groom change into their 'going away' outfits at the end of the reception, before leaving for their wedding night or honeymoon. The type of outfits chosen is entirely personal, and will vary according to whether the couple are travelling straight to their honeymoon destination by car, train or plane, or leave the evening reception to go to a local hotel for their wedding night (or are even staying the night at the reception hotel).

The bride may choose to leave in a traditional suit or dress and jacket, trouser suit, casual wear, summer frock or jeans, and the groom should decide on his outfit accordingly. Make arrangements for the clothes, with shoes, underwear and accessories, to be taken and left safely at the reception venue, and ensure that there is a room available in which the bride and groom can get changed before going away. Nowadays, many couples stay late at the evening 'do' and decide to depart for the wedding night in morning or lounge suit and wedding dress. Whatever the final decision, make sure that 'someone' will collect the wedding dress, morning suit and other wedding clothes (from reception venue or honeymoon hotel) the next day, after the couple have left for their honeymoon.

Civil Ceremony

Choice of dress for the new civil ceremony is completely free. Provided it doesn't offend the Registrar, and the arrangements comply with the marriage laws, you have a free hand. You can opt for a traditional white wedding, with yards of bridesmaids, and groom and best man in toppers and tails, or wear a 'posh frock' or suit, or even fancy dress costume, as for a Register Office wedding.

You could stage a black tie event, as is popular in the States, with the bride in a wedding or ball gown, and the guests in evening dress. How about getting married in mediaeval court dress, wonderful for a wedding in an ancient castle, followed by a mediaeval banquet for the reception, or a gauzy, flowing Empire style gown for a summer wedding held in a stately home? You could have a sailor theme for a wedding on a moored boat, or a masked ball or fancy dress themed party in a hotel. The possibilities are endless, and as long as you make it clear on the invitations what the guests are expected to wear, the day should be great fun for everyone.

Wedding dresses can be bought, made or hired as for a church or Register Office wedding, while clothes for a special themed wedding can be bought, made professionally or at home, or hired from a theatrical costumier or dress hire shop.

PART SIX
Travel &
Accommodation

22

"GET ME TO THE CHURCH
ON TIME"

Every bride has her childhood dream of driving to church on her wedding day in a beautiful limousine or horse drawn carriage, wearing a fairytale dress and surrounded by flowers and wedding ribbons. This can still happen, and usually does if you want it to, but the bride may have to come down to earth to sort out the practicalities first!

Besides transport for the bride and her father to the ceremony, and for the bride and groom from ceremony to reception, transport has to be arranged for the bridesmaids, pageboys and bride's mother, groom and best man and groom's parents, either in wedding cars or their own transport. Arrangements must also be made to ensure that all the guests without their own cars can get to the church and be given a lift to the reception. Bride and groom will also need transport when they leave on their honeymoon, unless spending their wedding night at the reception hotel, and for their honeymoon journey after the wedding night.

Wedding Cars and Carriages
'You pay your money and take your pick' – prices will rise according to the level of luxury and/or fantasy you want or are willing to pay for. The bride can choose to walk to church if she

lives within a *very short* walking distance of the church/Register Office *and reception*, or the reception is being held at her home. If the bride is wearing a traditional wedding dress this is really only practical in summer, and even then plenty of large golf umbrellas should be to hand for the wedding entourage 'just in case'!

If you are watching the expenses there is no need to hire a 'proper wedding car' provided there is a reliable family car available, and a reliable friend or member of the family is willing to act as chauffeur for the day. On the practical side, this car needs to be of a reasonable size with four doors, in order to allow the bride graceful access and adequate space, particularly if she is wearing a full skirted dress or a long train – try getting that in and out of a two door Mini Metro (no, please don't!). Many people use mini-cabs or taxis, and bookings should be made in advance, to make sure the car(s) will be available at exactly the right time on the day, and will be suitable to carry the bride and bridesmaids – make sure the firm appreciate the cars are for a wedding when you book.

Check parking and waiting restrictions outside the church or Register Office; parking may be easy enough in a country lane, but can be difficult outside a city church or many Register Offices. The cars may have to be parked elsewhere and return for the bridal party after the ceremony. The Register Office ceremony is relatively short, but church weddings are longer and vary according to the type of service, so check times with the Registrar or clergyman to make sure the cars will be there to collect the bride and groom after the service.

Specialist Wedding Car Services
These are available in most districts. You can find local firms from adverts in the local press, via Yellow Pages or at Wedding Fayres. Telephone the company to find out what cars are available, and visit the garage to look at the cars and make sure they will be satisfactory.

Wedding cars are traditionally large, luxurious limousines, the kind of car that most of us don't travel in very often – Rolls Royce, Daimler and Mercedes are the most usual. The cars are generally black, grey or white, but if you want a particular colour you may have to search around. Check if the car will be decorated with ribbons (usually white, but you may have a special colour scheme in mind), and ask whether there will be flowers, fresh, silk or dried, on the back window shelf. Ask what the driver will wear – chauffeur's uniform, a suit or (hopefully not) jeans and a sweater! These limos provide plenty of room for the bride and her finery, and ensure that she will arrive, uncreased, in style and comfort.

If the bride's (or more often the groom's) dream car is something special or unusual – a Silver Cadillac, an open Rolls Royce convertible, an enormous 1950's American gas guzzler, a Vintage Silver Ghost or a wonderful veteran car from the early 1900s – these can be found, if you're lucky, by word of mouth from friends or your local garage. There are cars kept by enthusiasts who will hire them out for weddings and drive the cars themselves, often in a very smart chauffeur's outfit to match the car. Again, these cars can also be found from advertisements in wedding magazines, Wedding Fayres, Wedding Shops and Yellow Pages. If you still can't find what you want, Talking Pages or specialist car magazines may have helpful information.

Take special care when choosing unusual cars, particularly the smaller veteran cars, that there is actually room for the bride to travel in them if she is wearing a 'big' dress. Open cars may look lovely on a hot sunny day, but aren't quite the same if it's raining, and even a short journey in an open car can cause havoc with the bridal hair-do and head-dress. Allow extra time for the journeys when using a veteran car, and if there is a long distance from church to reception a veteran car may not be a practical proposition.

A Horse and Carriage
Romantic couples may choose to travel by horse and carriage, and here again you can find details of companies who will supply this kind of transport from wedding magazines and Fayres, Yellow Pages or even by enquiring at the local stables. An open carriage can look absolutely stunning, but it is wise to ensure that there is a hood available in case of wet weather, and a horse-drawn vehicle may not be practical if there are long journeys involved.

Booking the Transport
If possible, go and look at the car or carriage you have chosen, sit in it and envisage the wedding finery spread around before

making the final choice. Book the transport as early as possible to make sure you can have what you want. Prices for the more unusual modes of transport will vary, but will generally be more expensive than the usual limousines, which will be dearer than 'normal' taxis or mini cabs. If your particular car or horse and carriage has to be brought from a distant part of the country, there will be even more costs involved, including overnight accommodation for driver and horses. Make sure you get full details of all the charges *in writing* when making the booking.

Most firms will require a deposit on booking and settlement in full either 7 days before the wedding or on the day itself. If you are paying on the day, have cheque or money ready beforehand, to be sure you can find it at the last minute – in an envelope in the bride's mother's wedding handbag is a good place, as she won't be going to the ceremony without it.

Sort out timetables and journey times, taking into account expected traffic conditions, especially if the marriage is taking place in a town centre on a Saturday. Local firms will be aware of any trouble spots on the route, but if you are hiring a car or a carriage from another area it would be wise to do a 'practice drive' to the church in the weeks before the wedding to get the timing right.

Church Wedding

Transport for the Bridesmaids

If you are not far from the church, most wedding cars can be used for two or even three journeys, with the bridesmaids and often the bride's mother being delivered before the bride and her father. However, if there is a long drive this will not be practical; the bridesmaids can't be left waiting for an hour at the church before the bride arrives. Also, if the bride is travelling in a special or veteran car (or by horse and carriage), the double journey will not be practical. In any of these situations you will need an additional car to take the bridesmaids and ensure that they arrive 10 minutes before the service. Some hire firms will provide this free with the bride's transport, others will make a charge. Alternatively, a relative or friend with a 'posh' car may be persuaded into service, or perhaps a car could be hired from a local car firm (but then you may still need 'someone' to act as the driver).

The Others

Having decided on the official wedding car(s) and transport for the bridal retinue, transport for the rest of the wedding party and the guests must be considered. Guests usually make their own way to the church (parking arrangements should be enclosed with the invitations if it is difficult), but you may need to arrange transport for elderly relatives with other members of the family.

The Groom and Best Man generally drive to church together, sometimes with a pre-arranged stop for a swift drink with the ushers en route! They should *arrive* at the church 30 minutes before the start of the service, and it is the best man's responsibility to make sure that they do. They often travel in the best man's car, or a taxi or mini cab should be arranged in advance.

The Ushers should get to the church at the same time, using their own transport or making their own way, so that they will be there before the guests, who should start arriving 15-20 minutes before the service. (The wedding photographer should also be there early, in order to take pictures of the groom, best man, ushers and wedding guests as they arrive.)

The Groom's Parents usually travel in their own car, but if they are elderly or do not drive, they may travel with the groom, or another relative or friend may drive them. Alternatively they can make arrangements in advance to travel by taxi or minicab.

The Bride's Mother usually travels with the bridesmaids and pageboys if there is room (particularly if there are young children in the bridal retinue), or she may travel with another friend or relative, arriving with the bridesmaids. They should all arrive about 10 minutes before the service to give the photographer time for informal shots of the group before the bride arrives.

The Bride and her Father (or whoever is giving her away) should arrive at the church exactly on time. Traditionally the bride is allowed to be late, but this can cause difficulties if there is another wedding following on, and think of the distraught groom worrying in the front pew and bridesmaids and guests getting fidgety, besides the discourtesy to the vicar, choir, organist and bell ringers. However, she should not be early either. The driver should 'cruise around' for a few minutes if necessary. By the time the bride has disembarked from the car, straightened her veil, kissed her mother goodbye and posed for photographs with her father, she will be a few minutes late entering the church anyway.

After the Service
The wedding car should pull up to the church door when it is indicated that the couple are ready to leave for the reception. The bride and groom are driven off in a flurry of (bird friendly) confetti, and the rest of the bridal retinue, family and guests follow to the reception. Some firms provide champagne in the wedding car to refresh bride and groom en route, but be aware that drinking champagne in a moving car while dressed in wedding finery is not easy and may not be such a good idea. If there is a second wedding car the bridesmaids and bride's mother will travel in this, as they came, and there may be room for the bride's father beside the driver, otherwise he can drive himself or get a lift with the best man or the groom's parents.

If you have only one wedding car, arrangements must be made for the bridesmaids and bride's parents to get to the reception. Often the bride's father's car is taken and parked near the church early in the day so that the bride's parents can drive themselves and some of the bridesmaids to the reception (don't forget to take the car keys to the wedding), or the adult bridesmaids can travel with the best man or their own parents or boyfriends. Little bridesmaids and pageboys will go with their own parents (who will have the necessary child seats in their cars). Alternatively the bride's parents can travel with the groom's parents or vice versa, or both sets of parents may need a lift with the best man or other relatives.

The parents, best man and chief bridesmaid should make sure that they arrive at the reception a few minutes after the bride and groom in order to greet the guests when they arrive. The rest of the wedding guests will usually make their own way to the reception, arrangements having been made in advance for any elderly or infirm guests, or anyone else without a car to be given a lift. The ushers are responsible for getting everyone away safely, even making extra trips in their own cars if necessary, and they should be the last to leave the church.

If a lot of guests have travelled to the wedding by plane, train or coach and so do not have their own transport, a minibus or coach could be hired to take guests to the church and on to the reception. Arrangements must be made in advance with the guests concerned so that everyone knows 'how they'll get there'. Firms with these vehicles to hire, with or without a driver, can be found at local taxi companies or through Yellow Pages, and will usually require a deposit on booking and full settlement a week in advance or on the day.

Register Office Wedding

The size of the wedding party attending the Register Office may have to be limited, as the office is often not very big and there is only room for immediate families and close friends to attend the ceremony, the rest of the guests being invited to the reception later.

If the bride is wearing a traditional wedding dress, she may choose to arrive in a wedding limousine with her father as for a church wedding, while groom, best man, groom's parents and other guests make their own way, either in their own cars or by taxi or minicab (booked in advance). The bride's mother may drive herself and other members of the family (possibly the bride's younger brothers and sisters) or can be driven by another relative. Bridesmaids can travel with the bride's mother or in a pre-arranged taxi or the wedding car if there is to be one, as for a church wedding. The same cars will then be used to take everyone to the reception, although of course bride and groom will travel together in the wedding car.

At a more informal wedding, the couple may arrive together in their own car, driven by themselves or a relative, or in a wedding car or taxi, which is then used to take them to the reception. Their families and friends will make their own way to the Register Office. Taxi bookings should be made in advance, to make sure everyone will arrive on time.

Most Register Offices are in or near town centres, where parking may be difficult or restricted altogether, so enquire about parking when you make the wedding arrangements with the Registrar. Wedding cars and taxis may be able to wait outside during the short ceremony, or they may have to 'drive round the block' and return at an agreed time – the driver will know what is the usual practice.

Service of Blessing

If the couple choose a Service of Blessing straight after the Register Office ceremony, they will travel on to it together in the car in which the bride arrived for the wedding. If the proceedings are very informal, the couple may choose to drive themselves in their own car. The Register Office guests should go ahead in their own transport, so that the bride and groom are the last to arrive and will enter the church for the service together, where the rest of the guests will have already assembled and be waiting for them. If there is a large number of guests at this service, transport to the reception will have to be organised for the wedding party and the guests as for a church wedding.

If the Service of Blessing is held on another day to the wedding, transport arrangements for the couple and their guests will have to be made as for a church wedding, but the couple will arrive together at the church after all the guests have assembled.

Civil Ceremony

Transport arrangements will vary according to how the couple want to plan the occasion. As with a Register Office wedding they may choose that the bride should arrive with her father in a big limousine, after the groom and wedding guests have assembled and the bridesmaids have arrived, in order to make a grand entrance on her father's arm followed by the bridal retinue. On the other hand the bride and groom may arrive together in the wedding car, or may be completely informal and drive together to the wedding in their own car. If the ceremony is taking place in a hotel, they may choose to stay there the previous night, so that there is no wedding journey to be arranged, apart from transport for any guests who are unable to make their own arrangements. The couple may decide to spend the wedding night at the wedding venue if it is suitable, or travel arrangements will have to be made for them after the reception.

Going Away

Traditionally the bride and groom change into their 'going away outfits' (in the bride's case this can attract almost as much attention as her wedding dress), and leave for their honeymoon in a decorated car trailing tin cans and old shoes for luck. Nowadays, with the growing popularity of an evening party, many couples spend their wedding night near, or at, the reception hotel, leaving for their honeymoon next morning.

Many hotels offer a 'Wedding Package' which includes the bridal suite for the wedding night and special room rates for wedding guests; a very attractive offer in these days of the breathalyser for those needing to drive home.

Leaving by Taxi
Bookings should be made in advance of the wedding day, especially if the couple are travelling on by train or plane and must get to the station or airport by a certain time. Warn the taxi company that the car is for newly weds, and they may be willing to decorate the car accordingly with 'Just Married' notices and balloons, but they will not appreciate any foam sprays used on the cars. The groom must make sure that in all the excitement he has cash, cheque book, credit cards and any travel tickets with him.

Leaving by Car
Unless the bride or groom is teetotal it would be extremely stupid even to contemplate driving themselves from the reception – glasses are refilled and toasts are drunk, and even half glasses can soon bring you over a safe limit. If you have a non-drinking friend it is well to ask in advance if he or she will act as chauffeur on the day, and drive the couple to their destination (hotel, station or airport), either in their own or the friend's car. Whatever car is used, the owner must be prepared for it to be well decorated – toilet paper streamers, balloons, shaving foam sprays, tin cans, old shoes and confetti inside and out – but the decorators (usually best man, ushers, bridesmaids and the couple's friends) should be asked in advance not to use anything that could damage the car (lipstick or wax crayons on windows or paintwork) and not to interfere with the engine or petrol or do anything that could be dangerous.

Make sure the car is filled with petrol and that the driver knows the way to the destination, and has a map and written directions if necessary, as nothing could be worse than missing the honeymoon plane or train, or driving round country lanes in the dark trying to find the honeymoon hotel! At our wedding the groom's uncle was unable to mix alcohol with his medication (much to his chagrin!) so he was 'volunteered' to drive the going away car, and did sterling work ferrying guests home too.

The guests should all make their own arrangements for travelling home, but both bride's and groom's parents should keep an eye on the proceedings as guests thank them and leave, making sure that anyone who ought not to be driving is given a lift or persuaded to take a taxi. It is helpful to look up the phone numbers of local taxi and minicab firms beforehand and keep that list handy (in the bride's mother's handbag?) in case it's needed.

If the couple are spending the night at a local hotel and will need their car the next day, it should be taken there the night before or early on the wedding morning by the groom and best man, who can then drive back in the best man's car. Of course, word may get out of the car's whereabouts, and the couple's friends may manage to sneak round and decorate the car accordingly, to give them a good send off to their married life!

Honeymoon Transport
If the couple do not leave directly on their honeymoon after the reception, but decide to spend their wedding night locally, they will need to make arrangements for their transport the next day. If they are going to travel in their own car or one lent by a friend or relative, that car will need to be parked at the wedding night hotel the day before or early on the wedding day, usually by the groom and best man. Make sure the groom then puts the car keys safely with his going away luggage, or even leaves a spare key at the hotel reception. If the couple are using a borrowed car, check the insurance as it may be necessary for the owner to pay a small extra premium to cover them too.

If the couple decide to hire a car, this should be booked in advance, to avoid any last minute disappointment. Arrangements should be made to collect the car, either on foot or by public transport (in which case you will have to leave the luggage at the hotel and return for it in the car), or by taxi, or the hire company may be able to deliver it to the hotel. Arrangements must also be made about returning the car (borrowed or hired) according to whether the couple are returning to that area after the honeymoon, or going directly to their own home in another part of the country.

If the couple are leaving next day by train or plane, arrangements for a taxi, hire car or lift to the station or airport should be made in advance.

23

ACCOMMODATION

Wedding Guests

Overnight accommodation for family and friends coming from a distance away should be arranged as early as possible in order to ensure that everyone who needs a bed for the night has somewhere to stay. If the bride, groom and their families live and work locally, this should not be too much of a problem, as most people will be able to go home after the reception, with beds being provided by members of the family or at local hotels or B&Bs for the few guests from away.

However, when one family (often the groom's) comes from another part of the country, or abroad, or the couple themselves live and work away from the home town where the wedding is taking place, or if the wedding is being held where the couple are living and both families have to travel to attend, accommodation can be a major headache. The bride, or her mother, should be very careful how many people are offered accommodation at the bride's house – remember the bride and the bridesmaids have first rights to the bathrooms! It is much more sensible to accept gratefully any hospitality offered by family and neighbours.

Check on the availability of rooms in local hotels, guest houses, pubs, B&Bs and even youth hostels and holiday flats, and if possible arrange overnight accommodation within walking distance of the reception, to facilitate getting back after the reception. (It will be easier to arrange lifts to the ceremony, if necessary, than lifts from the party later.) If the reception is being held at a hotel, rooms may be available there for the night, possibly at a special rate, for wedding guests. If you know guests are likely to need to stay overnight, before and/or after the wedding, but will expect to make their own arrangements, you could include details of this and other locally available accommodation with their wedding invitations.

If you book overnight hotel accommodation for your guests, unless you intend to foot the hotel bill yourself, make it quite clear to the hotel who is going to pay, and if possible ensure that any deposits are paid directly by the guests themselves to avoid any misunderstandings later. This may seem petty, but hotel or even B&B bills for a large number of people can be very expensive, and once a firm booking is made, the deposit at least is non returnable, and some hotels will expect to be paid in full even if the guest is eventually unable to attend the wedding. Bear in mind that although some of the guests (possibly the older generation) may enjoy a night in a luxurious hotel or even make it an excuse for a long weekend away, even B&Bs can be an expensive item for a whole family with young children, or the younger friends of the bride and groom, so any accommodation offered by friends and neighbours will be very welcome.

At 'our wedding', with half the wedding guests, including the bride's family, coming from abroad, a real boon was the loan of her complete house by a kind neighbour who was unfortunately to be away on holiday over the wedding weekend. This provided free beds for eight impecunious young people, including the best man, who had already had the expense of their air fares from Germany. I filled the fridge and cupboard with breakfast cereals, milk, bacon, eggs, bread, butter and marmalade, showed them where the tea and coffee were to be found, and left them to cater for themselves at breakfast time. I booked up all the village B&Bs within walking distance of the church and reception, with hotel rooms for the more luxuriously inclined, and a complete farmhouse and holiday complex for the bride, her parents and immediate family, so that the bride's mother could help her daughter prepare for her wedding as she would have done at home.

Wedding Night Arrangements

With the ever increasing popularity of the evening reception, many couples choose to stay and enjoy the fun until late at night, instead of departing on their honeymoon in the afternoon or early evening as used to be the norm not so long ago. The couple then spend their wedding night locally, and leave for the honeymoon at their leisure next day.

If the reception is being held at a hotel, a night in the bridal suite may be included in the wedding package. This solves any problems of a wedding journey late at night, although some couples may prefer to be on their own, and would rather not find themselves having breakfast next morning in the company of other wedding guests who also stayed at the hotel overnight. The bride and groom may decide to spend their wedding night in secret at a local hotel, or to splash out on a night of luxury at a famous or really super (and generally extremely expensive) hotel, either in the heart of town or in a secluded country location.

All hotel reservations should be made as early as possible, especially during the summer when popular hotels get very booked up. If you ask for the bridal suite, or let the hotel know that the booking is for newly weds (although they'll probably guess anyway!), complimentary flowers, fruit, champagne, chocolates and breakfast in bed may be provided by the management. If the booking is made several months ahead, it is wise to confirm it nearer the date, even if a deposit has been paid, with approximate arrival time and any special requirements the couple would like.

PART SEVEN
Doing & Paying

24

THE JOB ROSTER
– WHO DOES WHAT

In the past, when most girls (and often young men, too) lived at home with their family until they got married, the bride's parents would assume responsibility for the wedding plans, and the arrangements would be made by the mother of the bride. Today, despite the fact that many girls live and work away from the family house before getting married, the majority of brides still 'come home' for their wedding, and although the bride and groom now usually plan their own wedding and may even make most of the arrangements, it is often still the bride's mother who is ultimately responsible for the actual running of the day.

Some couples, often those who have been living together for some time, those embarking on a second marriage, or older couples, do choose to organise their own wedding completely, from sending out the invitations to paying the final bills, just leaving the mother of the bride to buy her own wedding outfit and arrive in the biggest hat on the day. Great!! If the couple organise their own wedding they will have to undertake the arrangements usually carried out by the bride's parents, although the father of the bride will still retain the privilege of escorting his daughter to the ceremony and giving her away at a church wedding.

Bride's Mother
The bride's mother acts as hostess for the day, particularly at the

wedding reception, and usually at the evening party unless this is specifically arranged by the couple themselves for their younger friends. In consultation with the bride and groom the bride's mother will:

1. Place engagement and wedding announcements in national and/or local papers.
2. Liaise with bride, groom and groom's parents to compile the guest list.
3. Order or buy invitations, write and despatch them.
4. Order or buy all necessary wedding stationery.
5. Book the Reception, discuss menus and all other details for the day. Confirm numbers of guests later.
6. Book the Evening Reception – arrange the catering and book the band and/or disco.
7. Book photographer and videocamera operator, if required.
8. Order flowers – bouquets and floral decorations.
9. Make or order the wedding cake.
10. Book wedding cars and check all transport arrangements.
11. Arrange overnight accommodation for guests, as needed.
12. Help compile and manage the wedding present list.
13. Help the bride to choose her wedding dress and other wedding finery, trousseau and bridesmaids' dresses.
14. Check hiring of morning suits, if appropriate.
15. Buy her own wedding outfit and a lovely hat.
16. On the day: help her daughter to dress and, if necessary, take charge of any little bridesmaids and pageboys on the way to the ceremony.
17. Stand first in the receiving line to greet the guests.
18. Arrange for the display of the wedding presents.

Bride

Although the mother of the bride is traditionally in charge of the wedding arrangements, most brides today are very involved with all aspects of the wedding plans. The bride will:

1. Choose the church, Register Office or civil venue where she would like to be married and meet the clergyman or Registrar with her fiancé to arrange the ceremony and fulfil all legal requirements.
2. Help compile guest lists for wedding and evening reception.
3. Help her mother, or assume responsibility for the rest of the wedding arrangements (see above).

4. Choose bridesmaids, flowergirls and pageboys.
5. Draw up the wedding present list and send thank-you letters as presents are received.
6. Choose and buy her wedding dress and accessories, going away outfit, honeymoon clothes and trousseau.
7. Choose bridesmaids' dresses and accessories and pageboys' outfits.
8. Discuss wedding hairstyles with her hairdresser.
9. Choose her wedding ring with her fiancé and buy a wedding ring for him if he is going to wear one.
10. Change her passport to her married name – allow adequate time for this to be done by the Passport Office.
11. Arrange the wedding rehearsal with the clergyman.
12. Arrange the Hen Party with her girlfriends.

Bride's Father

Besides traditionally paying for almost everything, he will:

1. Buy or hire his wedding outfit.
2. Attend the wedding rehearsal.
3. Travel with his daughter to the ceremony and escort her down the aisle if a church wedding.
4. Escort the groom's mother to the vestry for the signing of the register, and escort her from the church.
5. May witness the wedding register.
6. Make sure that the bride's mother and himself get to the reception before the guests arrive, and stand in the receiving line to greet them.
7. Make the first speech at the reception and propose the toast to the bride and groom.

If the bride's father is dead, incapacitated, unavailable or unable to attend the wedding, these duties are usually undertaken by a male relative of the bride – brother, uncle, cousin, or son in the case of a marriage between an older couple. If the bride's parents are divorced, it will be a personal matter for the bride as to whether her father is invited to the wedding, and, if the bride's mother has remarried, the bride will have to decide whether to ask her stepfather or her own father to give her away, according to family circumstances. There is no reason why the bride may not ask a female relative – mother, aunt, sister or daughter – to accompany her if necessary, provided the clergyman is aware of the arrangement.

Chief Bridesmaid (single) or Matron of Honour (married)

The bride can ask whoever she likes to assist her on her wedding day in this role, but she usually chooses a sister, cousin, best friend or the groom's sister for the honour. If the bride has several sisters it may be more tactful to ask a friend, to save any bad feelings among the unselected ones! An older bride, or a bride marrying for the second time, particularly if she is not wearing a traditional wedding dress, may choose to be attended by just one married friend, also wearing a day dress or suit with a pretty hat. The chief bridesmaid/matron of honour will:

1. Help the bride to choose the bridesmaids' outfits.
2. Arrange the Hen Party, with the bride's help.
3. Attend the wedding rehearsal.
4. Help the bride to dress and check that all the going away luggage is packed and taken to the right place.
5. Marshal the bridesmaids and pageboys before they leave for the ceremony; supervise the little ones if necessary.
6. Arrange the bride's dress when she alights from the wedding car before entering the church/Register Office.
7. Stand behind the bride during the ceremony, hold her bouquet and arrange the bridal veil when it is lifted.
8. Follow the bride into the vestry escorted by the best man.
9. May witness the signing of the register.
10. Walk down the aisle behind the bridesmaids, escorted by the best man.
11. Pose for photographs with the wedding party.
12. May stand in the receiving line at the reception.
13. Help the bride to change into her going away outfit.

Bridesmaids

The bride can choose as many bridesmaids as she likes from amongst the relatives and friends of herself and the groom, bearing in mind that they will have to stand and walk together as a group, so should be matched by height and age if possible although this can be very difficult to achieve, and the bride may decide that the people involved are more important than the final effect. Be wary of choosing too many tiny tots, who may get bored and disrupt the service. A great deal of tact may be needed when choosing bridesmaids, especially if the couple both come from large families, but it must be remembered that it is 'the bride's day' and she should make the final choice. The bridesmaids' duties are mainly decorative, to provide a pretty background retinue for the bride. They will:

1. Possibly help to choose the bridesmaids' outfits.
2. Assist the bride to dress, if necessary.
3. Dress little bridesmaids and pageboys, if necessary, and supervise or amuse them, making sure they stay clean and tidy until they leave for the ceremony.
4. Walk behind the bride up the aisle, at a church wedding, and carry the train, if appropriate.
5. Supervise little ones in the vestry during the signing of the register.
6. Walk from the church behind the bride and groom, and *look decorative* in the photographs.
7. If it's rainy or wet underfoot, help the bride to keep the wedding dress clear of the puddles when walking into church/Register Office or leaving for the reception.

Flowergirls
Traditionally these are very young bridesmaids who carry a small basket of flowers or flower petals. Very tiny tots may need to be encouraged to walk into church behind the bride and in front of the older bridesmaids, and to stand or sit quietly during the service (large kneelers could be placed at the side of the aisle for them to sit on, or they could join their parents in adjacent pews during the actual marriage service). The flowergirls go into the vestry with the bridal retinue during the signing of the register, and then walk down the aisle in front of the bride and groom, strewing flowers in their path (it is best to check with the vicar that this is acceptable when first arranging the service). They may attend the wedding rehearsal, or practise at home instead.

Pageboys
Because weddings are 'so soppy', the age limit for pageboys is usually fixed at 7 or 8 (and that's pushing it a bit!). The boys must be taught to walk quietly into church, without pushing and shoving, especially if there are also little bridesmaids in the entourage. They walk behind the bride, carrying her train as necessary. They go into the vestry for the signing of the register, and walk from the church behind the bride as before. The

pageboys may attend the wedding rehearsal, and/or practise with the train before the day.

Bridegroom

Traditionally the groom was mostly concerned with paying the few expenses for which the bride's father was not responsible, but today he is likely to be much more involved with making the actual wedding arrangements as well as footing certain bills. He will:

1. Buy the engagement ring (a wise man takes his fiancée with him to buy this!!!).
2. Make an appointment for himself and the bride to meet the clergyman or Registrar, to arrange the marriage ceremony and fulfil the necessary legalities.
3. Pay for the marriage licence, Registrar's fees, if appropriate, and all church expenses – clergy fees, choir, organist, bellringers and verger. If possible pay all fees in advance to save 'settling up' on the day.
4. Choose the best man and ushers.
5. Decide on the wedding attire for himself and chief male guests (best man, ushers and both fathers), and make sure they all know what to wear.
6. Organise his own wedding outfit (hiring morning suit if necessary), including shirt, shoes, tie, socks and underwear, and also his going away outfit and honeymoon clothes.
7. Buy the wedding ring(s) with his fiancée (but the bride pays for the groom's ring if he has one).
8. Pay for the bouquets, buttonholes and corsages, although they are usually chosen by the bride.
9. Buy thank-you presents for the bridesmaids, pageboys and best man and ushers.
10. Organise and attend the Stag Night.
11. Book and pay for accommodation for the wedding night and for the honeymoon.
12. Park his own car at the wedding night hotel before the wedding. Arrange going away and honeymoon transport.
13. Attend the wedding rehearsal.
14. Arrive early at the church (30 minutes before the ceremony), greet the guests and the clergyman and sit in the front right-hand pew to await the bride.
15. Stand in the receiving line at the reception.

16. Make a speech at the reception on behalf of his wife and himself, and propose a toast to the bridesmaids.
17. Open the dancing at the evening reception by leading his bride onto the floor for the first dance.

Best Man

A reliable, traditionally unmarried, relative (often a brother or cousin) or close friend of the groom. It is helpful if the best man knows at least some of the guests, and makes himself familiar with the area in which the wedding is taking place, in order to be able to direct the guests to the church/Register Office and reception as necessary. He acts as a minder/valet/chauffeur to the groom before the ceremony, and may be appointed toast-master/master of ceremonies at the reception. The best man will:

1. Organise the Stag Night with the groom, and make sure the groom gets home safely.
2. Organise own wedding outfit, check the groom has his ready, and that the buttonholes have been ordered.
3. Check transport arrangements to take himself and the groom to ceremony, and to take bride and groom to their wedding night and/or honeymoon destination. Go with the groom to leave his car at the wedding night hotel.
4. Check arrangements for the honeymoon luggage, passports, tickets, etc.
5. Attend the wedding rehearsal.
6. Help the groom to dress, collect and/or deliver buttonholes for groom, himself, ushers and possibly groom's father.
7. Organise the ushers and make sure the service sheets are taken to the church.
8. Get the groom to the church 30 minutes early, sit with him in the front right-hand pew until the bride arrives, then stand on the groom's right during the marriage service.
9. Take care of the wedding ring(s) and produce them without a fuss at the right time in the service.
10. Escort the chief bridesmaid/matron of honour into the vestry and then back down the aisle.
11. Possibly witness the signing of the register.
12. Make sure arrangements are made to get all the guests to the reception, and delegate this responsibility to the ushers.
13. May stand in the receiving line at the reception.
14. May act as toastmaster or master of ceremonies.

15. Make a speech in response to the toast to the bridesmaids.
16. Read out telemessages and cards (carefully censoring any unsuitable for public reading).
17. Collect groom's wedding outfit after wedding, and return it to hire shop with his own (and others), if appropriate.
18. Make sure bride and groom get safely away for their wedding night, with all their necessary travel documents, passports, tickets, visas, money, car keys and luggage.

Ushers
Chosen by the bridegroom, ushers are usually young, unmarried male relatives or friends of the bride and groom – it is useful to have ushers from 'both sides' as they will then recognise guests from both families. The ushers should wear similar outfits to groom and best man, with buttonholes provided by the groom. The ushers will:

1. Organise, hire or buy their own wedding outfits.
2. Arrive at the church before or with the groom and best man (30 minutes before the service).
3. It may be necessary for one or more ushers to supervise parking arrangements outside the church/Register Office.
4. Collect the service sheets from the best man, or get out the hymn books, and put some ready for use by the bridal retinue at the end of the front pews.
5. Greet guests as they arrive, give them a service sheet, ask if are 'bride or groom' and show them to their places. Relatives and friends of the bride sit on the left facing the altar, those of the groom on the right. Immediate family sit in the front pews; the very front left pew is left empty for the bride's mother. If one 'side' is out numbered, guests can be asked to fill in the empty pews on the other side.
6. Escort the bride's mother to her place in the front left hand pew.
7. Check transport arrangements for all the guests from ceremony to reception, and make sure everyone is given a lift if necessary. One or more ushers may need to go ahead to supervise parking arrangements at the reception, but the others do not leave the church until all the guests have left.

25

THE GRAND TOTAL – WHO PAYS WHAT!

Traditionally the bride's parents pay for practically everything (fine if you have a family of sons), apart from a few bills for which the bridegroom takes responsibility. Nowadays many families share the costs, especially if one family is better off than the other, or the groom has a much larger family to invite than the bride. It is becoming much more common for the bride and groom to make a contribution or to pay for their own wedding, although this is more usual when the couple are already living together or when it is a second marriage.

Bride's Parents

The bride's parents pay for:

1. The wedding announcements.
2. Invitations, service sheets and all wedding stationery.
3. The reception and catering, including all food and drink, unless a pay bar has been arranged and guests buy some of their own drinks.
4. The evening reception – this may include the food and all drinks or just a welcome drink with guests buying from the bar for the rest of the evening.
5. The wedding cake.
6. Photographer and videocamera operator, and their own wedding photographs and album.
7. Flowers and decorations for church and reception, and for their own home.
8. May pay for overnight accommodation for immediate family or other guests, but this is not expected.

9. Wedding cars or transport for the bridal retinue to ceremony and reception.
10. The wedding dress, head-dress and accessories (but nowadays the bride usually pays for these herself).
11. Outfits for bridesmaids and pageboys (although they often pay for their own outfits, or their parents do!).
12. Going away outfit, honeymoon clothes and trousseau for the bride (but usually the bride of today will pay for these herself).
13. They may pay for the hire of morning suits for impecunious best man and ushers, but this should not necessarily be expected.
14. Their own wedding outfits, with the biggest and best hat at the wedding for the mother of the bride!

Bridegroom

The bridegroom pays for:

1. The engagement ring.
2. The marriage licence, Registrar's fees and/or all church expenses – clergy fees, choir, organist, bell ringers and verger.
3. Wedding ring for the bride.
4. All the bouquets, buttonholes and corsages.
5. Presents for bridesmaids, pageboys, best man and ushers.
6. May pay for the Stag Night, or the cost may be shared by all the participants (or the others may pay for the bridegroom!).
7. His own wedding outfit, going away and honeymoon clothes.
8. Wedding night accommodation and the honeymoon.
9. The bride and groom's own wedding album and photographs.

Bride

The bride pays for:

1. Wedding ring for the groom, if worn.
2. Often pays for her wedding dress and accessories, going away outfit, honeymoon clothes and trousseau.
3. May pay for the Hen Party, or the cost may be shared (or the girls may pay for her).

Groom's Parents
The groom's parents may offer to make a contribution or to share the cost of the wedding with the bride's parents. The bride's father may welcome this, or still insist on paying for everything himself.

Best Man and Ushers
The best man and the ushers will often buy or pay for the hire of their own wedding outfits, although these may be paid for by the parents of bride or groom.

Bridesmaids and Pageboys
The outfits and accessories for the bride's attendants are traditionally paid for by the bride or her parents, but many bridesmaids, or parents of younger bridesmaids and pageboys, now offer to pay for their own outfits (or make a contribution towards the cost).

APPENDIX

CHECKLISTS

Checklist for the Wedding Stationery

Wedding Invitations
Evening Reception Invitations } allow 4-6 weeks for printing (send 8-12 weeks ahead)

Service/Hymn Sheets } allow 4-6 weeks for printing

Place cards
Menu cards
Seating plan
Printed napkins
    coasters
    books of matches
Wedding cake boxes
Thank-you cards
} allow 4-6 weeks for printing
or
buy as early as possible
(but don't forget where
you've stored them!)

Checklist for the Wedding Cake

If buying, order from the hotel, restaurant or caterer with the food for the reception, or order it from a baker or private professional decorator.

If you're making your own:

2-3 months ahead – make the cake(s)

4-6 weeks ahead – marzipan the cake(s)

2-3 weeks ahead – ice the cake(s)

1 week ahead – put the final touches to the decoration

Number of slices per size of cake

Square	cm	12.5	15	17.5	20	22.5	25	27.5	30	32.5
	in	5	6	7	8	9	10	11	12	13
Round or	cm	15	17.5	20	22.5	25	27.5	30	32.5	35
Horseshoe	in	6	7	8	9	10	11	12	13	14
Approx. no. of pieces		16	20	28	36	48	72	92	120	136

Make arrangements for the display of the cake at the reception
and ensure that the stand, knife, table and cloth are available.

Checklist for the Floral Dance

Bouquets   – bride
                           bridesmaids
                           flowergirls

Floral head-dresses – bride
                           bridesmaids
                           flowergirls

Buttonholes   – groom
                           best man
                           ushers
                           bride's father
                           groom's father
                           principal male guests
                                    (grandfathers, uncles)

Corsages   – bride's mother
                           groom's mother
                           principal lady guests
                                    (grandmothers, aunts)

Church/Register Office flower arrangements
Flower decorations at the reception (indoors and outside)
Flowers for the top of the wedding cake
Flower arrangements in bride's/bride's mother's house
Garden flowers in the bride's mother's garden.

TIMETABLE FOR 'THE DAY'

In the Morning

Groom and best man park the groom's car at the wedding night hotel (if necessary), returning together in the best man's car. 'Someone' takes bride and groom's going away clothes to the reception, and *hangs them up* ready to wear, and leaves the honeymoon luggage there or takes it to the wedding night hotel. (All this could be done the night before.)

Bouquets, buttonholes and corsages should be delivered to the bride's home (or to where she is getting ready for the ceremony).

The best man collects buttonholes from the bride's house for distribution to the groom, ushers and groom's father.

Church Wedding

60 mins before the service:
   photographer to bride's house, if arranged

35 mins before the service:
   photographer arrives at church

30 mins before the service:
   groom, best man and ushers arrive at church (groom with best man, ushers in own transport)

15-20 mins before service:
   groom's parents and guests arrive at church
   (own transport or arranged lifts)

10-15 mins before service:
   groom, best man and guests take places inside church
   bride's mother arrives (either with bridesmaids in wedding car or driven by relative or friend) and is escorted to her seat by an usher

10 mins before the service:
   bridesmaids and pageboys arrive (in wedding car) and pose for photographs

On time:
>bride and her father arrive (in the wedding car), pose briefly for photographs and enter the church, followed by the bridal retinue

Marriage service takes place (approximately 45 minutes)

Marriage party pose for photographs after the service before leaving for the reception in the following order:
>bride and groom
>bridesmaids and pageboys
>bride's parents and groom's parents
>best man (possibly with chief bridesmaid)
>wedding guests
>ushers

Register Office Wedding (and Service of Blessing)

5-10 mins before the ceremony:
>invited family and guests, groom's parents, bride's mother and possibly bride's father arrive

2-3 mins before the ceremony:
>groom and best man arrive; bridesmaids arrive; bride arrives with her father, or bride and groom arrive together

On time:
>bride and groom meet the Registrar in private where the Registrar will explain the proceedings; family and guests now enter the wedding room

Marriage ceremony proceeds (approximately 15-20 minutes)

After the ceremony the bride and groom may pose very briefly for photographs in the office, but must then pose outside for further pictures.

If followed by a formal reception, the couple leave first, followed by the bridesmaids, both sets of parents, best man and the guests as at a church wedding.

If there is to be a Service of Blessing, the family and guests will hurry ahead to take their places in the church, so that everyone is seated before the bride and groom arrive and enter the church together for the service (which lasts approximately 25-30 minutes).

TRANSPORT AFTER CEREMONY

To The Reception

Occupants	*Vehicle*
Bride and Groom	Wedding car

Bridesmaids Bride's mother Bride's father (if room) }	Second wedding car, if used, or bride's father goes with best man

Or

Bride's parents Groom's parents }	Own cars, or together, or arranged lift or with best man

Adult bridesmaids	With bride/groom's parents, own parents, boyfriends or best man

Little bridesmaids Pageboys }	With own parents (don't forget the child seats if necessary)

Best man	Own transport (may take others)

Wedding guests	Own transport or lifts arranged in advance

Ushers	Own transport (may take others)

After the Reception

Occupants	*Vehicle*
Bride and Groom	Own car/friend's car (driven by non-drinking friend) or taxi
Wedding guests	Own transport or taxi

Bride and Groom's Honeymoon Transport
Own car, borrowed car or self-drive hired car or taxi, hire car or
lift to station or airport.

INDEX